S0-AJA-673

THE PATHS OF INLAND COMMERCE

EXTRA-ILLUSTRATED EDITION

∵

VOLUME 21
THE CHRONICLES
OF AMERICA SERIES
ALLEN JOHNSON
EDITOR

GERHARD R. LOMER
CHARLES W. JEFFERYS
ASSISTANT EDITORS

Philada. to Pittsburgh 20 Days.

Gravure, Anderson-Lamb Co N.Y.

A CONESTOGA WAGON

Photograph from the original in the National Museum,
Washington.

THE PATHS OF INLAND COMMERCE

A CHRONICLE OF
TRAIL, ROAD, AND WATERWAY
BY ARCHER B. HULBERT

NEW HAVEN: YALE UNIVERSITY PRESS
TORONTO: GLASGOW, BROOK & CO.
LONDON: HUMPHREY MILFORD
OXFORD UNIVERSITY PRESS

THE LIBRARY
COLBY JUNIOR COLLEGE
NEW LONDON, N. H.

E
773
C56
vol. 21

Copyright, 1920, by Yale University Press

13863

PREFACE

If the great American novel is ever written, I hazard the guess that its plot will be woven around the theme of American transportation, for that has been the vital factor in the national development of the United States. Every problem in the building of the Republic has been, in the last analysis, a problem in transportation. The author of such a novel will find a rich fund of material in the perpetual rivalries of pack-horseman and wagoner, of riverman and canal boatman, of steamboat promoter and railway capitalist. He will find at every point the old jostling and challenging the new: pack-horsemen demolishing wagons in the early days of the Alleghany traffic; wagoners deriding Clinton's Ditch; angry boatmen anxious to ram the paddle wheels of Fulton's *Clermont*, which threatened their monopoly. Such opposition has always been an incident of progress; and even in this new country, receptive as it was to new ideas, the Washingtons, the Fitches, the Fultons, the Coopers, and the Whitneys, who saw visions and dreamed dreams, all had to face scepticism and hostility from those whom they would serve.

A. B. H.

Worcester, Mass.,
    June, 1919.

CONTENTS

ILLUSTRATIONS

THE PATHS OF INLAND COMMERCE

CHAPTER I

THE MAN WHO CAUGHT THE VISION

INLAND America, at the birth of the Republic, was as great a mystery to the average dweller on the Atlantic seaboard as the elephant was to the blind men of Hindustan. The reports of those who had penetrated this wilderness — of those who had seen the barren ranges of the Alleghanies, the fertile uplands of the Unakas, the luxuriant blue-grass regions, the rich bottom lands of the Ohio and Mississippi, the wide shores of the inland seas, or the stretches of prairie increasing in width beyond the Wabash — seemed strangely contradictory, and no one had been able to patch these reports together and grasp the real proportions of the giant inland empire that had become a part of the United States. It was a pathless desert; it was a maze

1

of trails, trodden out by deer, buffalo, and Indian. Its great riverways were broad avenues for voyagers and explorers; they were treacherous gorges filled with the plunder of a million floods. It was a rich soil, a land of plenty; the natives were seldom more than a day removed from starvation. Within its broad confines could dwell a great people; but it was as inaccessible as the interior of China. It had a great commercial future; yet its gigantic distances and natural obstructions defied all known means of transportation.

Such were the varied and contradictory stories told by the men who had entered the portals of inland America. It is not surprising, therefore, that theories and prophecies about the interior were vague and conflicting nor that most of the schemes of statesmen and financiers for the development of the West were all parts and no whole. They all agreed as to the vast richness of that inland realm and took for granted an immense commerce therein that was certain to yield enormous profits. In faraway Paris, the ingenious diplomat, Silas Deane, writing to the Secret Committee of Congress in 1776, pictured the Old Northwest — bounded by the Ohio, the Alleghanies, the Great Lakes, and the Mississippi — as paying the whole expense of the Revolutionary War.[1] Thomas Paine in 1780 drew specifications for a State of from twenty to thirty millions of acres lying west of Virginia and south of the Ohio River, the sale of which land would pay the cost of three years of the war.[2] On the other hand, Pelatiah Webster, patriotic economist that he was, decried in 1781 all schemes to "pawn" this vast westward region; he likened such plans to "killing the goose that laid an egg every day, in order to tear out at once all that was in her belly." He advocated the township system of compact and regular settlement; and he argued that any State making a cession of land would reap great benefit "from the produce and trade" of the newly created settlements.

There were mooted many other schemes. General Rufus Putnam, for example, advocated the

[1] Deane's plan was to grant a tract two hundred miles square at the junction of the Ohio and the Mississippi to a company on the condition that a thousand families should be settled on it within seven years. He added that, as this company would be in a great degree commercial, the establishing of commerce at the junction of those large rivers would immediately give a value to all the lands situated on or near them.

[2] Paine thought that while the new State could send its exports southward down the Mississippi, its imports must necessarily come from the East through Chesapeake Bay because the current of the Mississippi was too strong to be overcome by any means of navigation then known.

Pickering or "Army" plan of occupying the West; he wanted a fortified line to the Great Lakes, in case of war with England, and fortifications on the Ohio and the Mississippi, in case Spain should interrupt the national commerce on these waterways. And Thomas Jefferson theorized in his study over the toy states of Metropotamia and Polypotamia — brought his

> . . . trees and houses out
> And planted cities all about.

But it remained for George Washington, the Virginia planter, to catch, in something of its actual grandeur, the vision of a Republic stretching towards the setting sun, bound and unified by paths of inland commerce. It was Washington who traversed the long ranges of the Alleghanies, slept in the snows of Deer Park with no covering but his greatcoat, inquired eagerly of trapper and trader and herder concerning the courses of the Cheat, the Monongahela, and the Little Kanawha, and who drew from these personal explorations a clear and accurate picture of the future trade routes by which the country could be economically, socially, and nationally united.

Washington's experience had peculiarly fitted him to catch this vision. Fortune had turned him westward as he left his mother's knee. First as a surveyor for Lord Fairfax in the Shenandoah Valley and later, under Braddock and Forbes, in the armies fighting for the Ohio against the French he had come to know the interior as it was known by no other man of his standing. His own landed property lay largely along the upper Potomac and in and beyond the Alleghanies. Washington's interest in this property was very real. Those who attempt to explain his early concern with the West as purely altruistic must misread his numerous letters and diaries. Nothing in his unofficial character shows more plainly than his business enterprise and acumen. On one occasion he wrote to his agent, Crawford, concerning a proposed land speculation: "I recommend that you keep this whole matter a secret or trust it only to those in whom you can confide. If the scheme I am now proposing to you were known, it might give alarm to others, and by putting them on a plan of the same nature, before we could lay a proper foundation for success ourselves, set the different interests clashing and in the end overturn the whole." Nor can it be denied that Washington's attitude to the commercial development of the West was characterized in his early days by a narrow colonial partisanship. He was a stout Virginian; and all stout Virginians of that day refused to admit the pretensions of other colonies to the land beyond the mountains.

But from no man could the shackles of self-interest and provincial rivalry drop more quickly than they dropped from Washington when he found his country free after the close of the Revolutionary War. He then began to consider how that country might grow and prosper. And he began to preach the new doctrine of expansion and unity. This new doctrine first appears in a letter which he wrote to the Marquis de Chastellux in 1783, after a tour from his camp at Newburg into central New York, where he had explored the headwaters of the Mohawk and the Susquehanna: "I could not help taking a more extensive view of the vast inland navigation of these United States [the letter runs] and could not but be struck by the immense extent and importance of it, and of the goodness of that Providence which has dealt its favors to us with so profuse a hand. Would to God we may have wisdom enough to improve them. I shall not rest contented till I have explored the Western country, and traversed those lines, or great part of them, which have given bounds to a new empire."

"The vast inland navigation of these United States!" It is an interesting fact that Washington should have had his first glimpse of this vision from the strategic valley of the Mohawk, which was soon to rival his beloved Potomac as an improved commercial route from the seaboard to the West, and which was finally to achieve an unrivaled superiority in the days of the Erie Canal and the Twentieth Century Limited.

We may understand something of what the lure of the West meant to Washington when we learn that in order to carry out his proposed journey after the Revolution, he was compelled to refuse urgent invitations to visit Europe and be the guest of France. "I found it indispensably necessary," he writes, "to visit my Landed property West of the Apalacheon Mountains. . . . One object of my journey being to obtain information of the nearest and best communication between Eastern & Western waters; & to facilitate as much as in me lay the Inland Navigation of the Potomack."

On September 1, 1784, Washington set out from Mount Vernon on his journey to the West. Even the least romantic mind must feel a thrill in picturing this solitary horseman, the victor of Yorktown, threading the trails of the Potomac, passing on by

Cumberland and Fort Necessity and Braddock's grave to the Monongahela. The man, now at the height of his fame, is retracing the trails of his boyhood — covering ground over which he had passed as a young officer in the last English and French war — but he is seeing the land in so much larger perspective that, although his diary is voluminous, the reader of those pages would not know that Washington had been this way before. Concerning Great Meadows, where he first saw the "bright face of danger" and which he once described gleefully as "a charming place for an encounter," he now significantly remarks: "The upland, East of the meadow, is good for grain." Changed are the ardent dreams that filled the young man's heart when he wrote to his mother from this region that singing bullets "have truly a charming sound." Today, as he looks upon the flow of Youghiogheny, he sees it reaching out its finger tips to Potomac's tributaries. He perceives a similar movement all along the chain of the Alleghanies: on the west are the Great Lakes and the Ohio, and reaching out towards them from the east, waiting to be joined by portage road and canal, are the Hudson, the Susquehanna, the Potomac, and the James. He foresees these streams bearing to the Atlantic ports the golden produce of the interior and carrying back to the interior the manufactured goods of the seaboard. He foresees the Republic becoming homogeneous, rich, and happy. "Open *all* the communication which nature has afforded," he wrote Henry Lee, "between the Atlantic States and the Western territory, and encourage the use of them to the utmost . . . and sure I am there is no other tie by which they will long form a link in the chain of Federal Union."

Crude as were the material methods by which Washington hoped to accomplish this end, in spirit he saw the very America that we know today; and he marked out accurately the actual pathways of inland commerce that have played their part in the making of America. Taking the city of Detroit as the key position, commercially, he traced the main lines of internal trade. He foresaw New York improving her natural line of communication by way of the Mohawk and the Niagara frontier on Lake Erie — the present line of the Erie Canal and the New York Central Railway. For Pennsylvania, he pointed out the importance of linking the Schuylkill and the Susquehanna and of opening the two avenues westward to Pittsburgh and to Lake Erie. In general, he thus forecast the Pennsylvania Canal

nd the Pennsylvania and the Erie railways. For
Maryland and Virginia he indicated the Potomac
route as the nearest for all the trade of the Ohio
Valley, with the route by way of the James and
the Great Kanawha as an alternative for the settlements on the lower Ohio. His vision here was realized in a later day by the Potomac and the Chesapeake and Ohio Canal, the Cumberland Road, the
Baltimore and Ohio Railway, and by the James-
Kanawha Turnpike and the Chesapeake and Ohio
Railway.

Washington's general conclusions are stated in a
summary at the end of his *Journal*, which was reproduced in his classic letter to Harrison, written
in 1784. His first point is that every State which
had water routes reaching westward could enhance
the value of its lands, increase its commerce, and
quiet the democratic turbulence of its shut-in pioneer communities by the improvement of its river
transportation. Taking Pennsylvania as a specific
example, he declared that "there are one hundred
thousand souls West of the Laurel Hill, who are
groaning under the inconveniences of a long land
transportation. . . . If this cannot be made easy
for them to Philadelphia . . . they will seek a
mart elsewhere. . . . An opposition on the part

of [that] government . . . would ultimately bring on a separation between its Eastern and Western settlements; towards which there is not wanting a disposition at this moment in that part of it beyond the mountains."

Washington's second proposal was the achievement of a new and lasting conquest of the West by binding it to the seaboard with chains of commerce. He thus states his point: "No well informed mind need be told that the flanks and rear of the United territory are possessed by other powers, and formidable ones too — nor how necessary it is to apply the cement of interest to bind all parts of it together, by one indissoluble bond — particularly the middle States with the Country immediately back of them — for what ties let me ask, should we have upon those people; and how entirely unconnected should we be with them if the Spaniards on their right or Great Britain on their left, instead of throwing stumbling blocks in their way as they do now, should invite their trade and seek alliances with them?"

Some of the pictures in Washington's vision reveal, in the light of subsequent events, an almost uncanny prescience. He very plainly prophesied the international rivalry for the trade of the Great

Lakes zone, embodied today in the Welland and the Erie canals. He declared the possibility of navigating with ocean-going vessels the tortuous two-thousand-mile channel of the Ohio and the Mississippi River; and within sixteen years ships left the Ohio, crossed the Atlantic, and sailed into the Mediterranean. His description of a possible insurrection of a western community might well have been written later; it might almost indeed have made a page of his diary after he became President of the United States and during the Whiskey Insurrection in western Pennsylvania. He approved and encouraged Rumsey's mechanical invention for propelling boats against the stream, showing that he had a glimpse of what was to follow after Fitch, Rumsey, and Fulton should have overcome the mighty currents of the Hudson and the Ohio with the steamboat's paddle wheel. His proposal that Congress should undertake a survey of western rivers for the purpose of giving people at large a knowledge of their possible importance as avenues of commerce was a forecast of the Lewis and Clark expedition as well as of the policy of the Government today for the improvement of the great inland rivers and harbors.

"The destinies of our country run east and west.

Intercourse between the mighty interior west and the sea coast is the great principle of our commercial prosperity." These are the words of Edward Everett in advocating the Boston and Albany Railroad. In effect Washington had uttered those same words half a century earlier when he gave momentum to an era filled with energetic but unsuccessful efforts to join with the waters of the West the rivers reaching inland from the Atlantic. The fact that American engineering science had not in his day reached a point where it could cope with this problem successfully should in no wise lessen our admiration for the man who had thus caught the vision of a nation united and unified by improved methods of transportation.

CHAPTER II

THE RED MAN'S TRAIL

For the beginnings of the paths of our inland commerce, we must look far back into the dim prehistoric ages of America. The earliest routes that threaded the continent were the streams and the tracks beaten out by the heavier four-footed animals. The Indian hunter followed the migrations of the animals and the streams that would float his light canoe. Today the main lines of travel and transportation for the most part still cling to these primeval pathways.

In their wanderings, man and beast alike sought the heights, the passes that pierced the mountain chains, and the headwaters of navigable rivers. On the ridges the forest growth was lightest and there was little obstruction from fallen timber; rain and frost caused least damage by erosion; and the winds swept the trails clear of leaves in summer and of snow in winter. Here lay the easiest paths for

14

the heavy, blundering buffalo and the roving elk
and moose and deer. Here, high up in the sun,
where the outlook was unobstructed and signal fires
could be seen from every direction, on the longest
watersheds, curving around river and swamp, ran
the earliest travel routes of the aboriginal inhabitants and of their successors, the red men of historic
times. For their encampments and towns these
peoples seem to have preferred the more sheltered
ground along the smaller streams; but, when they
fared abroad to hunt, to trade, to wage war, to seek
new material for pipe and amulet, they followed in
the main the highest ways.

If in imagination one surveys the eastern half
of the North American continent from one of the
strategic passageways of the Alleghanies, say from
Cumberland Gap or from above Kittanning Gorge,
the outstanding feature in the picture will be
the Appalachian barrier that separates the interior
from the Atlantic coast. To the north lie the
Adirondacks and the Berkshire Hills, hedging New
England in close to the ocean. Two glittering
waterways lie east and west of these heights — the
Connecticut and the Hudson. Upon the valleys
of these two rivers converged the two deeply worn
pathways of the Puritan, the Old Bay Path

and the Connecticut Path.   By way of Westfield River, that silver tributary which joins the Connecticut at Springfield, Massachusetts, the Bay Path surmounted the Berkshire highlands and united old Massachusetts to the upper Hudson Valley near Fort Orange, now Albany.

Here, north of the Catskills, the Appalachian barrier subsides and gives New York a supreme advantage over all the other Atlantic States — a level route to the Great Lakes and the West. The Mohawk River threads the smiling landscape; beyond lies the "Finger Lake country" and the valley of the Genesee.   Through this romantic region ran the Mohawk Trail, sending offshoots to Lake Champlain and the St. Lawrence, to the Susquehanna, and to the Allegheny.   A few names have been altered in the course of years — the Bay Path is now the Boston and Albany Railroad, the Mohawk Trail is the New York Central, and Fort Orange is Albany — and thus we may tell in a dozen words the story of three centuries.

Upon Fort Orange converged the score of land and water pathways of the fur trade of our North. These Indian trade routes were slowly widened into colonial roads, notably the Mohawk and Catskill turnpikes, and these in turn were transformed into the Erie, Lehigh, Nickel Plate, and New York Central railways. But from the day when the canoe and the keel boat floated their bulky cargoes of pelts or the heavy laden Indian pony trudged the trail, the routes of trade have been little or nothing altered.

Traversing the line of the Alleghanies southward, the eye notes first the break in the wall at the Delaware Water Gap, and then that long arm of the Susquehanna, the Juniata, reaching out through dark Kittanning Gorge to its silver playmate, the dancing Conemaugh. Here amid its leafy aisles ran the brown and red Kittanning Trail, the main route of the Pennsylvania traders from the rich region of York, Lancaster, and Chambersburg. On this general alignment the *Broadway Limited* flies today toward Pittsburgh and Chicago. A little to the south another important pathway from the same region led, by way of Carlisle, Bedford, and Ligonier, to the Ohio. The "Highland Trail" the Indian traders called it, for it kept well on the watershed dividing the Allegheny tributaries on the north from those of the Monongahela on the south.

Farther to the south the scene shows a change, for the Atlantic plain widens considerably. The Potomac River, the James, the Pedee, and the Savannah flow through valleys much longer than

2

those of the northern rivers. Here in the South
commerce was carried on mainly by shallop and
pinnace. The trails of the Indian skirted the
rivers and offered for trader and explorer passage-
way to the West, especially to the towns of the
Cherokees in the southern Alleghanies or Unakas;
but the waterways and the roads over which the
hogsheads of tobacco were rolled (hence called
"rolling roads") sufficed for the needs of the thin
fringes of population settled along the rivers. Trails
from Winchester in Virginia and Frederick in
Maryland focused on Cumberland at the head of
the Potomac. Beyond, to the west, the finger tips
of the Potomac interlocked closely with the Monongahela and Youghiogheny, and through this network of mountain and river valley, by the "Shades
of Death" and Great Meadows, coiled Nemacolin's
Path to the Ohio. Even today this ancient route
is in part followed by the Baltimore and Ohio and
the Western Maryland Railway.

A bird's-eye view of the southern Alleghanies
shows that, while the Atlantic plain of Virginia and
the Carolinas widens out, the mountain chains increase in number, fold on fold, from the Blue Ridge
to the ragged ranges of the Cumberlands. Few
trails led across this manifold barrier. There was

a connection at Balcony Falls between the James River and the Great Kanawha; but as a trade route it was of no such value to the men of its day as the Chesapeake and Ohio system over the same course is to us. As in the North, so in the South, trade avoided obstacles by taking a roundabout, and often the longest route. In order to double the extremity of the Unakas, for instance, the trails reached down by the Valley of Virginia and New River to the uplands of the Tennessee, and here, near Elizabethton, they met the trails leading up the Broad and the Yadkin rivers from Charleston, South Carolina.

To the west rise the somber heights of Cumberland Gap. Through this portal ran the famous "Warrior's Path," known to wandering hunters, the "trail of iron" from Fort Watauga and Fort Chiswell, which Daniel Boone widened for the settlers of Kentucky. To the southwest lay the Blue Grass region of Tennessee with its various trails converging on Nashville from almost every direction. Today the Southern Railway enters the "Sapphire Country," in which Asheville lies, by practically the same route as the old Rutherfordton Trail which was used for generations by red man and pioneer from the Carolina coast.

In our entire region of the Appalachians, from the Berkshire Hills southward, practically every old-time pathway from the seaboard to the trans-Alleghany country is now occupied by an important railway system, with the exception of the Warrior's Trail through Cumberland Gap to central Ohio and the Highland Trail across southern Pennsylvania. And even Cumberland Gap is accessible by rail today, and a line across southern Pennsylvania was once planned and partially constructed only to be killed by jealous rivals.

These numerous keys to the Alleghanies were a challenge to the men of the seaboard to seize upon the rich trade of the West which had been early monopolized by the French in Canada. But the challenge brought its difficult problems. What land canoes could compete with the flotillas that brought their priceless cargoes of furs each year to Montreal and Quebec? What race of landlubbers could vie with the picturesque bands of fearless *voyageurs* who sang their songs on the Great Lakes, the Ohio, the Illinois, and the Mississippi?

In the solution of this problem of diverting trade probably the factor of greatest importance, next to open pathways through the mountain barriers, was the rich stock-breeding ground lying between

the Delaware and the Susquehanna rivers, a region
occupied by the settlers familiarly known as the
Pennsylvania Dutch. In this famous belt, run-
ing from Pennsylvania into Virginia, originated the
historic pack-horse trade with the "far Indians"
of the Ohio Valley. Here, in the first granary of
America, Germans, Scotch-Irish, and English bred
horses worthy of the name. "Brave fat Horses" an
amazed officer under Braddock called the mounts
of five Quakers who unexpectedly rode into camp
as though straight "from the land of Goshen."
These animals, crossed with the Indian "pony"
from New Spain, produced the wise, wiry, and
sturdy pack-horse, fit to transport nearly two hundred pounds of merchandise across the rough and
narrow Alleghany trails. This animal and the heavy
Conestoga horse from the same breeding ground
revolutionized inland commerce.

The first American cow pony was not without
his cowboy. Though the drivers were not all of
the same type and though the proprietors, so
to speak, of the trans-Alleghany pack-horse trade
came generally from the older settlements, the bulk
of the hard work was done by a lusty army of men
not reproduced again in America until the picturesque figure of the cow-puncher appeared above

the western horizon.   This breed of men was nur-
tured on the outer confines of civilization, along the
headwaters of the Susquehanna, the Potomac, the
James, and the Broad — the country of the "Cow-
pens." Rough as the wilderness they occupied,
made strong by their diet of meat and curds, these
Tatars of the highlands played a part in the commercial history of America that has never had its
historian.   In their knowledge of Indian character,
of horse and packsaddle lore, of the forest and its
trails in every season, these men of the Cowpens
were the kings of the old frontier.

An officer under Braddock has left us one of the
few pictures of these people[1]:

From the Heart of the Settlements we are now got
into the Cow-pens; the Keepers of these are very ex-
traordinary Kind of Fellows, they drive up their Herds
on Horseback, and they had need do so, for their Cattle
are near as wild as Deer; a Cow-pen generally consists
of a very large Cottage or House in the Woods, with
about four-score or one hundred Acres, inclosed with
high Rails and divided; a small Inclosure they keep for
Corn, for the family, the rest is the Pasture in which
they keep their calves; but the Manner is far different
from any Thing you ever saw; they may perhaps have
a Stock of four or five hundred to a thousand Head of
Cattle belonging to a Cow-pen, these run as they please

[1] *Extracts of Letters from an Officer* (London, 1755).

in the Great Woods, where there are no Inclosures to
stop them.   In the Month of March the Cows begin
to drop their Calves, then the Cow-pen Master, with
all his Men, rides out to see and drive up the Cows with
all their new fallen Calves; they being weak cannot run
away so as to escape, therefore are easily drove up, and
the Bulls and other Cattle follow them; and they put
these Calves into the Pasture, and every Morning and
Evening suffer the Cows to come and suckle them,
which done they let the Cows out into the great Woods
to shift for their Food as well as they can; whilst the
Calf is sucking one Tit of the Cow, the Woman of the
Cow-Pen is milking one of the other Tits, so that she
steals some Milk from the Cow, who thinks she is giving it to the Calf; soon as the Cow begins to go dry, and
the Calf grows Strong, they mark them, if they are
Males they cut them, and let them go into the Wood.
Every Year in September and October they drive up
the Market Steers, that are fat and of a proper Age,
and kill them; they say they are fat in October, but I
am sure they are not so in May, June and July; they
reckon that out of 100 Head of Cattle they can kill
about 10 or 12 steers, and four or five Cows a Year; so
they reckon that a Cow-Pen for every 100 Head of
Cattle brings about £40 Sterling per Year.   The
Keepers live chiefly upon Milk, for out of their Vast
Herds, they do condescend to tame Cows enough to
keep their Family in Milk, Whey, Curds, Cheese and
Butter; they also have Flesh in Abundance such as it
is, for they eat the old Cows and lean Calves that are
like to die.   The Cow-Pen Men are hardy People, are
almost continually on Horseback, being obliged to
know the Haunts of their Cattle.

You see, Sir, what a wild set of Creatures Our English Men grow into, when they lose Society, and it is surprising to think how many Advantages they throw away, which our industrious Country-Men would be glad of: Out of many hundred Cows they will not give themselves the trouble of milking more than will maintain their Family.

With such a race of born horsemen, every whit as bold and resourceful as the *voyageurs*, to bear the brunt of a new era of transportation, all that was needed to challenge French trade beyond the Alleghanies was competent and aggressive leadership. The situation called for men of means, men of daring, men closely in touch with governors and assemblies and acquainted with the web of politics that was being spun at Philadelphia, Williamsburg, New York, London, and Paris. Generations of tenacious struggle along the American frontier had developed such men. The Weisers, Croghans, Gists, Washingtons, Franklins, Walkers, and Cresaps were men of varied descent and nationality. They had the cunning, the boldness, and the resources to undertake successfully the task of conquering commercially the Great West. They were the first men of the colonies to be unafraid of that bugbear of the trader, Distance. We may aptly call them the first Americans because, though not a few were actually born abroad, they were the first whose plans, spirit, and very life were dominated by the vision of an America of continental dimensions. The long story of French and English rivalry and of the war which ended it concerns us here chiefly as a commercial struggle. The French at Niagara (1749) had access to the Ohio by way of Lake Erie and any one of several rivers — the Allegheny, the Muskingum, the Scioto, or the Miami. The main routes of the English were the Nemacolin and Kittanning paths. The French, laboring under the disadvantages of the longer distance over which their goods had to be transported to the Indians and of the higher price necessarily demanded for them, had to meet the competition of the traders from the rival colonies of Pennsylvania and Virginia, each of them jealous of and underbidding the other.

When Céloron de Blainville was sent to the Allegheny in 1749, by the Governor of New France, his message was that "the Governor of Canada desired his children on Ohio to turn away the English Traders from amongst them and discharge them from ever coming to trade there again, or on any of the Branches." He sent away all the traders whom he found, giving them letters addressed to their respective governors denying England's right to trade in

the West.   To offset this move, within two years
Pennsylvania sent goods to the value of nine hundred pounds in order to hold the Indians constant.
The Governor had already ordered the traders to
sell whiskey to the Indians at "5 Bucks" per cask
and had told the Indians, through his agent Con-
rad Weiser, that if any trader refused to sell the
liquor at that price they might "take it from him
and drink it for nothing."   There was but one way
for the French to meet such competition.   Without
delay they fortified the Allegheny and began to
coerce the natives.   Driving away the carpenters
of the Ohio Company from the present site of Pittsburgh, they built Fort Duquesne.   The beginning
of the Old French War ended what we may call the
first era of the pack-horse trade.

The capture of Fort Duquesne by the English
army under General Forbes in 1758 and the final
conquest of New France two years later removed
the French barrier and opened the way to expansion beyond the Alleghanies. Thereafter settlements in the Monongahela country grew apace.
Pittsburgh, Uniontown, Morgantown, Brownsville,
Ligonier, Greensburg, Connellsville — we give the
modern names — became centers of a great migration which was halted only for a season by Pontiac's

Rebellion, the aftermath of the French War, and was resumed immediately on the suppression of that Indian rising. The pack-horse trade now entered its final and most important era. The earlier period was one in which the trade was confined chiefly to the Indians; the later phase was concerned with supplying the needs of the white man in his rapidly developing frontier settlements. Formerly the principal articles of merchandise for the western trade were guns, ammunition, knives, kettles, and tools for their repair, blankets, tobacco, hatchets, and liquor. In the new era every known product of the East found a market in the thriving communities of the upper Ohio. As time went on the West began to send to the East, in addition to skins and pelts, whiskey that brought a dollar a gallon. Each pony could carry sixteen gallons and every drop could be sold for real money. On the return trip the pack-horses carried back chiefly salt and iron.

Doddridge's *Notes*, one of the chief sources of our information, gives this lively picture:

In the fall of the year, after seeding time, every family formed an association with some of their neighbors, for starting the little caravan. A master driver was to be selected from among them, who was to be assisted by one or more young men and sometimes a boy or two. The horses were fitted out with pack-saddles, to the latter part of which was fastened a pair of hobbles made of hickory withes, — a bell and collar ornamented their necks. The bags provided for the conveyance of the salt were filled with bread, jerk, boiled ham, and cheese furnished a provision for the drivers. At night, after feeding, the horses, whether put in pasture or turned out into the woods, were hobbled and the bells were opened. The barter for salt and iron was made first at Baltimore; Frederick, Hagerstown, Oldtown, and Fort Cumberland, in succession, became the places of exchange. Each horse carried two bushels of alum salt, weighing eighty-four pounds to the bushel. This, to be sure, was not a heavy load for the horses, but it was enough, considering the scanty subsistence allowed them on the journey. The common price of a bushel of alum salt, at an early period, was a good cow and a calf.

Thus, with the English flag afloat at Fort Pitt, as Duquesne was renamed after its capture, a new day dawned for the great region to the West. Beyond the Alleghanies and as far as the Rockies, a new science of transportation was now to be learned — the art of finding the dividing ridge. Here the first routes, like the "Great Trail" from Pittsburgh to Detroit, struck out with an assurance that is in marvelous agreement with the findings of the surveyors of a later day. The railways, when they came, found the valleys and penetrated with their tunnels the watersheds from the heads of the streams of one drainage area to the streams of another. Thus on the Pennsylvania, the Baltimore and Ohio, the Southern, the Chesapeake and Ohio, and other railroads, important tunnels are to be found lying immediately under the Red Man's trail which clung to the long ascending slope and held persistently to the dividing ridges.

Even this necessarily brief survey shows plainly how that preëminently American institution, the ridge road, came about. East and west, it was the legitimate and natural successor to the ancient trail. With the coming of the wagon, whose rattle was heard among the hills as early as Braddock's campaign, the process of lowering these paths from the heights was inevitably begun, and it was to the riverways that men first looked for a solution of the difficult problems of inland commerce. Eventually the paths of inland commerce constituted a vast network of canals, roads, and railway lines in those very valleys to which Washington had called the nation's attention in 1784.

CHAPTER III

THE MASTERY OF THE RIVERS

It would perhaps have been well, in the light of later difficulties and failures, if the men who at Washington's call undertook to master the capricious rivers of the seaboard had studied a stately Spanish decree which declared that, since God had not made the rivers of Spain navigable, it were sacrilege for mortals to attempt to do so. Even before the Revolution, Mayor Rhodes of Philadelphia was in correspondence with Franklin in London concerning the experiences of European engineers in harnessing foreign streams. That sage philosopher, writing to Rhodes in 1772, uttered a clear word of warning: "rivers are ungovernable things," he had said, and English engineers "seldom or never use a River where it can be avoided." But it was the birthright of New World democracy to make its own mistakes and in so doing to prove for itself the errors of the Old World.

As energetic men all along the Atlantic Plain now took up the problem of improving the inland rivers, they faced a storm of criticism and ridicule that would have daunted any but such as Washington and Johnson of Virginia or White and Hazard of Pennsylvania or Morris and Watson of New York. Every imaginable objection to such projects was advanced — from the inefficiency of the science of engineering to the probable destruction of all the fish in the streams. In spite of these discouragements, however, various men set themselves to form in rapid succession the Potomac Company in 1785, the Society for Promoting the Improvement of Inland Navigation in 1791, the Western Inland Lock Navigation Company in 1792, and the Lehigh Coal Mine Company in 1793. A brief review of these various enterprises will give a clear if not a complete view of the first era of inland water commerce in America.

The Potomac Company, authorized in 1785 by the legislatures of Maryland and Virginia, received an appropriation of $6666 from each State for opening a road from the headwaters of the Potomac to either the Cheat or the Monongahela, "as commissioners . . . shall find most convenient and beneficial to the Western settlers." This was the only public aid which the enterprise received; and the stipulated purpose clearly indicates the fact that, in the minds of its promoters, the transcontinental character of the undertaking appeared to be vital.   The remainder of the money required for the work was raised by public subscription in the principal cities of the two States.   In this way £40,300 was subscribed, Virginia men taking 266 shares and Maryland men 137 shares.   The stockholders elected George Washington as president of the company, at a salary of thirty shillings a year, with four directors to aid him, and they chose as general manager James Rumsey, the boat mechanician.   These men then proceeded to attack the chief impediments in the Potomac — the Great Falls above Washington, the Seneca Falls at the mouth of Seneca Creek, and the Shenandoah Falls at Harper's Ferry.   But, as they had difficulty in obtaining workmen and sufficient liquor to cheer them in their herculean tasks, they made such slow progress that subscribers, doubting Washington's optimistic prophecy that the stock would increase in value twenty per cent, paid their assessments only after much deliberation or not at all.   Thirty-six years later, though $729,380 had been spent and lock canals had been opened about the unnavigable stretches of the Potomac River, a commission appointed to examine the affairs of the company reported "that the floods and freshets nevertheless gave the only navigation that was enjoyed." As for the road between the Potomac and the Cheat or the Monongahela, the records at hand do not show that the money voted for that enterprise had been used.

The Potomac Company nevertheless had accomplished something: it had acquired an asset of the greatest value — a right of way up the strategic Potomac Valley; and it had furnished an object lesson to men in other States who were struggling with a similar problem. When, as will soon be apparent, New York men undertook the improvement of the Mohawk waterway there was no pattern of canal construction for them to follow in America except the inadequate wooden locks erected along the Potomac. It is interesting to know that Elkanah Watson, prominent in inland navigation to the North, went down from New York in order to study these wooden locks and that New Yorkers adopted them as models, though they changed the material to brick and finally to stone.

Pennsylvania had been foremost among the colonies in canal building, for it had surveyed as early

3

13863

THE LIBRARY
COLBY JUNIOR COLLEGE
NEW LONDON, N. H.

as 1762 the first lock canal in America, from near Reading on the Schuylkill to Middletown on the Susquehanna. Work, however, had to be suspended when Pontiac's Rebellion threw the inland country into a panic. But the enterprise of Maryland and Virginia in 1785 in developing the Potomac aroused the Pennsylvanians to renewed activity. The Society for Promoting the Improvement of Roads and Inland Navigation set forth a programme that was as broad as the Keystone State itself. Their ultimate object was to capture the trade of the Great Lakes. "If we turn our view," read the memorial which the Society presented to the Legislature, "to the immense territories connected with the Ohio and Mississippi waters, and bordering on the Great Lakes, it will appear . . . that our communication with those vast countries (considering Fort Pitt as the port of entrance upon them) is as easy and may be rendered as cheap, as to any other port on the Atlantic tide waters."

Pennsylvania, lying between Virginia and New York, occupied a peculiar position. Her Susquehanna Valley stretched northwest — not so directly west as did the Potomac on the south and the Mohawk on the north. This more northerly trend led these early Pennsylvania promoters to believe

that, while they might "only have a share in
the trade of those [the Ohio] waters," they could
absolutely secure for themselves the trade of the
Great Lakes, "taking Presq' Isle [Erie, Pennsyl-
vania] which is within our own State, as the great
mart or place of embarkation."

The plan which the Society proposed involved the
improvement of water and land routes by way of the
Delaware to Lake Ontario and Lake Otsego, and of
eight routes by the Susquehanna drainage, north,
northwest, and west. A bill which passed the Legislature on April 13, 1791, appropriated money for
these improvements. Work was begun immediately on the Schuylkill-Susquehanna Canal, but
only four miles had been completed by 1794, when
the Lancaster Turnpike directed men's attention
to improved highways as an alternative more likely
than canals to provide the desired facilities for inland transportation. The work on the canal was
renewed, however, in 1821, when the rival Erie
Canal was nearing completion, and was finished in
1827. It became known as the Union Canal and
formed a link in the Pennsylvania canal system,
the development of which will be described in a
later chapter.

In New York State, throughout the period of the

Old French and the Revolutionary wars, barges and keel boats had plied the Mohawk, Wood Creek, and the Oswego to Lake Ontario. Around such obstructions as Cohoes Falls, Little Falls, and the portage at Rome to Wood Creek, wagons, sleds, and pack-horses had transferred the cargoes. To avoid this labor and delay men soon conceived of conquering these obstacles by locks and canals. As early as 1777 the brilliant Gouverneur Morris had a vision of the economic development of his State when "the waters of the great western inland seas would, by the aid of man, break through their barriers and mingle with those of the Hudson."

Elkanah Watson was in many ways the Washington of New York. He had the foresight, patience, and persistence of the Virginia planter. His *Journal* of a tour up the Mohawk in 1788 and a pamphlet which he published in 1791 may be said to be the ultimate sources in any history of the internal commerce of New York. As a result, a company known as "The President, Directors, and Company of the Western Inland Lock Navigation in the State of New York," with a capital stock of $25,000, was authorized by act of legislature in March, 1792, and the State subscribed for $12,500 in stock. Many singular provisions were inserted

in this charter, but none more remarkable than one
which stipulated that all profits over fifteen per
cent should revert to the State Treasury.   This
hint concerning surplus profits, however, did not
cause a stampede when the books were opened for
subscriptions in New York and Albany.   In later
years, when the Erie Canal gave promise of a new
era in American inland commerce, Elkanah Watson recalled with a grim satisfaction the efforts of
these early days.   The subscription books at the
old Coffee House in New York, he tells us, lay open
three days without an entry, and at Lewis's tavern
in Albany, where the books were opened for a similar period, "no mortal" had subscribed for more
than two shares.

The system proposed for the improvement of the
waterways of New York was similar to that projected for the Potomac.   A canal was to be cut
from the Mohawk to the Hudson in order to avoid
Cohoes Falls; a canal with locks would overcome
the forty-foot drop at Little Falls; another canal
over five thousand feet in length was to connect
the Mohawk and Wood Creek at Rome; minor improvements were to be made between Schenectady
and the mouth of the Schoharie; and finally the
Oswego Falls at Rochester were to be circumvented

also by canal.   All the objections, difficulties, and discouragements which had attended efforts to improve waterways elsewhere in America confronted these New York promoters.   They began in 1793 at Little Falls but were soon forced to cease owing to the failure of funds.   Under the encouraging spur of a state subscription to two hundred shares of stock, they renewed their efforts in 1794 but were again forced to abandon the work before the year had passed.   By November, 1795, however, they had completed the canal and in thirty days had received toll to the amount of about four hundred dollars.

The total actual work done is not clearly shown by the documents, but it is evident that the measure of success achieved was not equaled elsewhere on similar improvements on a large scale.   From 1796 to 1804 the tolls received at Rome amounted to over fifteen thousand dollars, and at Little Falls to over fifty-eight thousand dollars — a sum which exceeded the original cost of construction.   Dividends had crept up from three per cent in 1798 to five and a half per cent in 1817, the year in which work was begun on the Erie Canal.

No struggle for the mastery of an American river matches in certain respects the effort of the

Lehigh Coal and Navigation Company to bridle the Lehigh and make it play its part in the commercial development of Pennsylvania. The failures and trials of the promoters of this company were no less remarkable than was the great success that eventually crowned the effort. In 1793 the Lehigh Coal Mine Company was organized and purchased some ten thousand acres in the Mauch Chunk anthracite region, nine miles from the Lehigh River. It then appropriated a sum of money to build a road from the mines to the river in the expectation that the State would improve the navigation of the waterway, for which, it has already been noted, an appropriation had been made in 1791, in accordance with the programme of the Society for Promoting the Improvement of Roads and Inland Navigation. Nothing was done, however, to improve the river, and the company, after various attempts at shipping coal to Philadelphia, gave up the effort and allowed the property, which was worth millions, to lie idle. In 1807 the Lehigh Coal Mine Company, in another effort to get its wares before the public, granted to Rowland and Butland, a private firm, free right to operate one of its veins of coal; but this operation also resulted in failure. In 1813 the company made a third attempt and granted to a private concern a lease of the entire property on the condition that ten thousand bushels of coal should be taken to market annually. Difficulties immediately made themselves apparent. No contractor could be found who would haul the output to the Lehigh River for less than four dollars a ton, and the man who accepted those terms lost money. Of five barges filled at Mauch Chunk three went to pieces on the way to Philadelphia. Although the contents of the other two sold for twenty dollars a ton, the proceeds failed to meet expenses, and the operating company threw up the lease.

But it happened that White and Hazard, the wire manufacturers who purchased this Lehigh coal, were greatly pleased with its quality. Believing that coal could be obtained more cheaply from Mauch Chunk than from the mines along the Schuylkill, White, Hauto, and Hazard formed a company, entered into negotiation with the owners of the Lehigh mines, and obtained the lease of their properties for a period of twenty years at an annual rental of one ear of corn. The company agreed, moreover, to ship every year at least forty thousand bushels of coal to Philadelphia for its own consumption, to prove the value of the property.

White and his partners immediately applied to the Legislature for permission to improve the navigation of the Lehigh, stating the purpose of the improvement and citing the fact that their efforts would tend to serve as a model for the improvement of other Pennsylvania streams. The desired opportunity "to ruin themselves," as one member of the Legislature put it, was granted by an act passed March 20, 1818. The various powers applied for, and granted, embraced the whole range of tried and untried methods for securing "a navigation downward once in three days for boats loaded with one hundred barrels, or ten tons." The State kept its weather eye open in this matter, however, for a small minority felt that these men would not ruin themselves. Accordingly, the act of grant reserved to the commonwealth the right to compel the adoption of a complete system of slack-water navigation from Easton to Stoddartsville if the service given by the company did not meet "the wants of the country."

Capital was subscribed by a patriotic public on condition that a committee of stockholders should go over the ground and pass judgment on the probable success of the effort. The report was favorable, so far as the improvement of the river was concerned; but the nine-mile road to the mines was unanimously voted impracticable. "To give you an idea of the country over which the road is to pass," wrote one of the commissioners, "I need only tell you that I considered it quite an easement when the wheel of my carriage struck a stump instead of a stone." The public mind was divided. Some held that the attempt to operate the coal mine was farcical, but that the improvement of the Lehigh River was an undertaking of great value and of probable profit to investors. Others were just as positive that the river improvement would follow the fate of so many similar enterprises but that a fortune was in store for those who invested in the Lehigh mines.

The direct result of the examiners' report and of the public debate it provoked was the organization of the first interlocking companies in the commercial history of America. The Lehigh Navigation Company was formed with a capital stock of $150,000 and the Lehigh Coal Company with a capital stock of $55,000. This incident forms one of the most striking illustrations in American history of the dependence of a commercial venture upon methods of inland transportation. The Lehigh Navigation Company proceeded to build its dams and walls while the Lehigh Coal Company constructed the first roadway in America built on the principle — later adopted by the railways — of dividing the total distance by the total descent in order to determine the grade. Not to be outdone in point of ingenuity, the Lehigh Navigation Company, then suffering from an unprecedented dearth of water, adopted White's invention of sluice gates connecting with pools which could be filled with reserve water to be drawn upon as navigation required. By 1819 the necessary depth of water between Mauch Chunk and Easton was obtained. The two companies were immediately amalgamated under the title of the Lehigh Coal and Navigation Company and by 1823 had sent over two thousand tons of coal to market.

As most of the efforts to improve the rivers, however, met with indifferent success and many failures were recorded, the pendulum of public confidence in this aid to inland commerce swung away, and highway improvement by means of stone roads and toll road companies came into favor in the interval between the nation's two eras of river improvement and canal building.

CHAPTER IV

A NATION ON WHEELS

In early days the Indian had not only followed the watercourses in his canoe but had made his way on foot over trails through the woods and over the mountains. In colonial days, Englishman and Frenchman followed the footsteps of the Indian, and as settlement increased and trade developed, the forest path widened into the highway for wheeled vehicles. Massachusetts began the work of road making in 1639 by passing an act which decreed that "the ways" should be six to ten rods wide "in common grounds," thus allowing sufficient room for more than one track. Similar broad "ways" were authorized in New York and Pennsylvania in 1664; stumps and shrubs were to be cut close to the ground, and "sufficient bridges" were to be built over streams and marshy places. Virginia passed legislation for highways at an early date, but it was not until 1662 that strict laws were enacted with a view to keeping the roads in a permanently good condition. Under these laws surveyors were appointed to establish in each county roads forty feet wide to the church and to the courthouse. In 1700, Pennsylvania turned her local roads over to the county justices, put the King's highway and the main public roads under the care of the governor and his council, and ordered each county to erect bridges over its streams.

The word "roadmaking" was capable of several interpretations. In general, it meant outlining the course for the new thoroughfare, clearing away fallen timber, blazing or notching the trees so that the traveler might not miss the track, and building bridges or laying logs "over all the marshy, swampy, and difficult dirty places."

The streams proved serious obstacles to early traffic. It has been shown already that the earliest routes of animal or man sought the watersheds; the trails therefore usually encountered one stream near its junction with another. At first, of course, fording was the common method of crossing water, and the most advantageous fording places were generally found near the mouths of tributary streams, where bars and islands are frequently formed and where the water is consequently shallow. When ferries began to be used, they were usually situated just above or below the fords; but when the bridge succeeded the ferry, the primitive bridge builder went back to the old fording place in order to take advantage of the shallower water, bars, and islands. With the advent of improved engineering, the character of river banks and currents was more frequently taken into consideration in choosing a site for a bridge than was the case in the olden times, but despite this fact the bridges of today, generally speaking, span the rivers where the deer or the buffalo splashed his way across centuries ago.

On the broader streams, where fording was impossible and traffic was perforce carried by ferry, the canoe and the keel boat of the earliest days gave way in time to the ordinary "flat" or barge. At first the obligation of the ferryman to the public, though recognized by English law, was ignored in America by legislators and monopolists alike. Men obtained the land on both sides of the rivers at the crossing places and served the public only at their own convenience and at their own charges. In many cases, to encourage the opening of roads or of ferries, national and state authorities made grants of land on the same principle followed in later days in the case of Western railroads. Such, for instance, was the grant to Ebenezer Zane, at Zanesville, Lancaster, and Chillicothe in the Northwest Territory. These monopolies some-times were extremely profitable: a descendant of the owners of the famous Ingles ferry across New River, on the Wilderness Road to Kentucky, is responsible for the statement that in the heyday of travel to the Southwest the privilege was worth from $10,000 to $15,000 annually to the family. But as local governments became more efficient, monopolies were abolished and the collection of tolls was taken over by the authorities. The awakening of inland trade is most clearly indi-cated everywhere by the action of assemblies re-garding the operation of ferries, and in general, by the beginning of the eighteenth century, tolls and ferries were being regulated by law.

But neither roads nor ferries were of themselves sufficient to put a nation on wheels. The early polite society of the settled neighborhoods traveled in horse litters, in sedan chairs, or on horseback, the women seated on pillions or cushions behind the saddle riders, while oxcarts and horse barrows brought to town the produce of the outlying farms. Although carts and rude wagons could be built entirely of wood, there could be no marked advance in transportation until the development of mining in certain localities reduced the price of iron. With the increase of travel and trade, the old world coach and chaise and wain came into use, and iron for tire and brace became an imperative necessity. The connection between the production of iron and the care of highways was recognized by legislation as early as 1732, when Maryland excused men and slaves in the ironworks from labor on the public roads, though by the middle of the century owners of ironworks were obliged to detail one man out of every ten in their employ for such work.

While the coastwise trade between the colonies was still preëminently important as a means of transporting commodities, by the beginning of the eighteenth century the land routes from New York to New England, from New York across New Jersey to Philadelphia, and those radiating from Philadelphia in every direction, were coming into general use. The date of the opening of regular freight traffic between New York and Philadelphia is set by the reply of the Governor of New Jersey in 1707 to a protest against monopolies granted on one of the old widened Indian trails between Burlington and Amboy. "At present," he says, "everybody is sure, *once a fortnight*, to have an opportunity of sending any quantity of goods, great or small, at reasonable rates, without being in danger of imposition; and the sending of this wagon is so far from being a grievance or monopoly, *that by this means and no other*, a trade has been carried on between Philadelphia, Burlington, Amboy, and New York, which was never known before."

The long Philadelphia Road from the Lancaster region into the Valley of Virginia, by way of Wadkins on the Potomac, was used by German and Irish traders probably as early as 1700. In 1728 the people of Maryland were petitioning for a road from the ford of the Monocacy to the home of Nathan Wickham. Four years later Jost Heydt, leading an immigrant party southward, broke open a road from the York Barrens toward the Potomac two miles above Harper's Ferry. This avenue — by way of the Berkeley, Staunton, Watauga, and Greenbrier regions to Tennessee and Kentucky — was the longest and most important in America during the Revolutionary period. The Virginia Assembly in 1779 appointed commissioners to view this route and to report on the advisability of making it a wagon road all the way to Kentucky.

4

In 1795, efforts were made in Kentucky to turn the Wilderness Trail into a wagon road, and in this same year the Kentucky Legislature passed an act making the route from Crab Orchard to Cumberland Gap a wagon road thirty feet in width.

From Pennsylvania and from Virginia commerce westward bound followed in the main the army roads hewn out by Braddock and Forbes in their campaigns against Fort Duquesne. In 1755, Braddock, marching from Alexandria by way of Fort Cumberland, had opened a passage for his artillery and wagons to Laurel Hill, near Uniontown, Pennsylvania. His force included a corps of seamen equipped with block and tackle to raise and lower his wagons in the steep inclines of the Alleghanies. Three years later, Forbes, in his careful, dogged campaign, followed a more northerly route. Advancing from Philadelphia and Carlisle, he established Fort Bedford and Fort Ligonier as bases of supply and broke a new road through the interminable forest which clothed the rugged mountain ranges. From the first there was bitter rivalry between these two routes, and the young Colonel Washington was roundly criticized by both Forbes and Bouquet, his second in command, for his partisan effort to "drive me down," as Forbes

phrased it, into the Virginia or Braddock's Road.
This rivalry between the two routes continued
when the destruction of the French power over the
roads in the interior threw open to Pennsylvania
and her southern neighbors alike the lucrative
trade of the Ohio country.

From the journals of the time may be caught faint
glimpses of the toils and dangers of travel through
these wild hill regions. Let the traveler of today,
as he follows the track that once was Braddock's
Road, picture the scene of that earlier time when, in
the face of every natural obstacle, the army toiled
across the mountain chains. Where the earth in
yonder ravine is whipped to a black froth, the
engineers have thrown down the timber cut in
widening the trail and have constructed a corduroy
bridge, or rather a loose raft on a sea of muck. The
wreck of the last wagon which tried to pass gives
some additional safety to the next. Already the
stench from the horse killed in the accident deadens
the heavy, heated air of the forest. The sailors,
stripped to the waist, are ready with ropes and
tackle to let the next wagon down the incline; the
pulleys creak, the ropes groan. The horses, weak
and terror-stricken, plunge and rear; in the final
crash to the level the leg of the wheel horse is

caught and broken; one of the soldiers shoots the animal; the traces are unbuckled; another beast is substituted. Beyond, the seamen are waiting with tackle attached to trees on the ridge above to assist the horses on the cruel upgrade — and Braddock, the deceived, maligned, misrepresented, and misjudged, creeps onward in his brave conquest of the Alleghanies in a campaign that, in spite of its military failure, deserves honorable mention among the achievements of British arms.

Everywhere, north and south, the early American road was a veritable Slough of Despond. Watery pits were to be encountered wherein horses were drowned and loads sank from sight. Frequently traffic was stopped for hours by wagons which had broken down and blocked the way. Thirteen wagons at one time were stalled on Logan's Hill on the York Road. Frightful accidents occurred in attempting to draw out loads. Jonathan Tyson, for instance, in 1792, near Philadelphia saw a horse's lower jaw torn off by the slipping of a chain. Save in the winter, when in the northern colonies snow filled the ruts and frost built solid bridges over the streams, travel on these early roads was never safe, rapid, nor comfortable. The comparative ease of winter travel for the carriage of heavy

freight and for purposes of trade and social intercourse gave the colder regions an advantage over
the southern that was an important factor in the
development of the country.

No genuine improvement of roads and highways
seems to have been attempted until the era her-
alded by Washington's letter to Harrison in 1784.
But the problem slowly forced itself upon all sections of the country, and especially upon Pennsylvania and Maryland, whose inhabitants began
to fear lest New York, Alexandria, or Richmond
should snatch the Western trade from Philadelphia
or Baltimore. The truth that underlies the prov-
erb that "history repeats itself" is well illustrated
by the fact that the first macadamized road in
America was built in Pennsylvania, for here also
originated the pack-horse trade and the Conestoga
horse and wagon; here the first inland American
canal was built, the first roadbed was graded on
the principle of dividing the whole distance by
the whole descent, and the first railway was operated. Macadam and Telford had only begun to
show the people of England how to build roads of
crushed stone — an art first developed by the French
engineer Trésaguet — when Pennsylvanians built
the Lancaster Turnpike. The Philadelphia and

Lancaster Turnpike Road Company was chartered April 9, 1792, as a part of the general plan of the Society for the Improvement of Roads and Inland Navigation already described. This road, sixty-two miles in length, was built of stone at a cost of $465,000 and was completed in two years. Never before had such a sum been invested in internal improvement in the United States. The rapidity with which the undertaking was carried through and the profits which accrued from the investment were alike astonishing. The subscription books were opened at eleven o'clock one morning and by midnight 2226 shares had been subscribed, each purchaser paying down thirty dollars. At the same time Elkanah Watson was despondently scanning the subscription books of his Mohawk River enterprise at Albany where "no mortal" had risked more than two shares.

The success of the Lancaster Turnpike was not achieved without a protest against the monopoly which the new venture created. It is true that in all the colonies the exercise of the right of eminent domain had been conceded in a veiled way to officials to whose care the laying out of roads had been delegated. As early as 1639 the General Court of Massachusetts had ordered each town to

choose men who, coöperating with men from the
adjoining town, should "lay out highways where
they may be most convenient, notwithstanding any
man's property, or any corne ground, so as it occasion not the pulling down of any man's house, or
laying open any garden or orchard." But the open
and extended exercise of these rights led to vigorous
opposition in the case of this Pennsylvania road.
A public meeting was held at the Prince of Wales
Tavern in Philadelphia in 1793 to protest in round
terms against the monopolistic character of the
Lancaster Turnpike. Blackstone and Edward III
were hurled at the heads of the "venal" legislators
who had made this "monstrosity" possible. The
opposition died down, however, in the face of the
success which the new road instantly achieved. The
Turnpike was, indeed, admirably situated. Converging at the quaint old "borough of Lancaster,"
the various routes — northeast from Virginia, east
from the Carlisle and Chambersburg region and
the Alleghanies, and southeast from the upper
Susquehanna country — poured upon the Quaker
City a trade that profited every merchant, land-
holder, and laborer. The nine tollgates, on the
average a little less than seven miles apart,
turned in a revenue that allowed the "President

and Managers" to declare dividends to stockholders running, it is said, as high as fifteen per cent.

The Lancaster Turnpike is interesting from three points of view: it began a new period of American transportation; it ushered in an era of speculation unheard of in the previous history of the country; and it introduced American lawmakers to the great problem of controlling public corporations.

Along this thirty-seven-foot road, of which twenty-four feet were laid with stone, the new era of American inland travel progressed. The array of two-wheeled private equipages and other family carriages, the stagecoaches of bright color, and the carts, Dutch wagons, and Conestogas, gave token of what was soon to be witnessed on the great roads of a dozen States in the next generation. Here, probably, the first distinction began to be drawn between the taverns for passengers and those patronized by the drivers of freight. The colonial taverns, comparatively few and far between, had up to this time served the traveling public, high and low, rich and poor, alike. But in this new era members of Congress and the élite of Philadelphia and neighboring towns were not to be jostled at the table by burly hostlers, drivers, wagoners, and hucksters. Two types of inns thus came quickly

into existence: the tavern entertained the stagecoach traffic, while the democratic roadhouse served
the established lines of Conestogas, freighters, and
all other vehicles which poured from every town,
village, and hamlet upon the great thoroughfare
leading to the metropolis on the Delaware. /

Among American inventions the Conestoga
wagon must forever be remembered with respect.
Originating in the Lancaster region of Pennsylvania and taking its name either from the horses of
the Conestoga Valley or from the valley itself, this
vehicle was unlike the old English wain or the
Dutch wagon because of the curve of its bed. This
peculiarly shaped bottom, higher by twelve inches
or more at each end than in the middle, made the
vehicle a safer conveyance across the mountains and
over all rough country than the old straight-bed
wagon. The Conestoga was covered with canvas, as were other freight vehicles, but the lines of
the bed were also carried out in the framework
above and gave the whole the effect of a great ship
swaying up and down the billowy hills. The
wheels of the Conestoga were heavily built and
wore tires four and six inches in width. The har-
ness of the six horses attached to the wagon was
proportionately heavy, the back bands being fifteen

inches wide, the hip straps ten, and the traces consisting of ponderous iron chains. The color of the original Conestoga wagons never varied: the underbody was always blue and the upper parts were red. The wagoners and drivers who manned this fleet on wheels were men of a type that finds no parallel except in the boatmen on the western rivers who were almost their contemporaries. Fit for the severest toil, weathered to the color of the red man, at home under any roof that harbored a demijohn and a fiddle, these hardy nomads of early commerce were the custodians of the largest amount of traffic in their day.

The turnpike era overlaps the period of the building of national roads and canals and the beginning of the railway age, but it is of greatest interest during the first twenty-five years of the nineteenth century, up to the time when the completion of the Erie Canal set new standards. During this period roads were also constructed westward from Baltimore and Albany to connect, as the Lancaster Turnpike did at its terminus, with the thoroughfares from the trans-Alleghany country. The metropolis of Maryland was quickly in the field to challenge the bid which the Quaker City made for western trade. The Baltimore-Reisterstown and

Baltimore-Frederick turnpikes were built at a cost
of $10,000 and $8000 a mile respectively; and
the latter, connecting with roads to Cumberland,
linked itself with the great national road to Ohio
which the Government built between 1811 and
1817. These famous stone roads of Maryland long
kept Baltimore in the lead as the principal outlet
for the western trade. New York, too, proved her
right to the title of Empire State by a marvelous activity in improving her magnificent strategic
position. In the first seven years of the nineteenth
century eighty-eight incorporated road companies
were formed with a total capital of over $8,000,000.
Twenty large bridges and more than three thousand miles of turnpike were constructed. The
movement, indeed, extended from New England to
Virginia and the Carolinas, and turnpike companies
built all kinds of roads — earth, corduroy, plank,
and stone.

In many cases the kind of road to be constructed,
the tolls to be charged, and the amount of profit to
be permitted, were laid down in the charters. Thus
new problems confronted the various legislatures,
and interesting principles of regulation were now
established. In most cases companies were allowed, on producing their books of receipts and

expenditures, to increase their tolls until they obtained a profit of six per cent on the investment, though in a number of cases nine per cent was permitted.   When revenues increased beyond the six per cent mark, however, the tendency was to reduce tolls or to use the extra profit to purchase the stock for the State, with the expectation of ultimately abolishing tollgates entirely.   The theories of state regulation of corporations and the obligations of public carriers, extending even to the compensation of workmen in case of accident, were developed to a considerable degree in this turnpike era; but, on the other hand, the principle of permitting fair profit to corporations upon public examination of their accounts was also recognized.

The stone roads, which were passable at all seasons, brought a new era in correspondence and business.   Lines of stages and wagons, as well known at that time as are the great railways of today, plied the new thoroughfares, provided some of the comforts of travel, and assured the safer and more rapid delivery of goods.   This period is sometimes known in American history as "The Era of Good Feeling" and the turnpike contributed in no small degree to make the phrase applicable not only to the domain of politics but to all the relations of social and commercial life.

While road building in the East gives a clear picture of the rise and growth of commerce and trade in that section, it is to the rivers of the trans-Alleghany country that we must look for a corresponding picture in this early period. The canoe and pirogue could handle the packs and kegs brought westward by the files of Indian ponies; but the heavy loads of the Conestoga wagons demanded stancher craft. The flatboat and barge therefore served the West and its commerce as the Conestoga and turnpike served the East.

CHAPTER V

THE FLATBOAT AGE

In the early twenties of the last century one of the popular songs of the day was *The Hunters of Kentucky*. Written by Samuel Woodworth, the author of *The Old Oaken Bucket*, it had originally been printed in the New York *Mirror* but had come into the hands of an actor named Ludlow, who was playing in the old French theater in New Orleans. The poem chants the praises of the Kentucky riflemen who fought with Jackson at New Orleans and indubitably proved

> That every man was half a horse
> And half an alligator.

Ludlow knew his audience and he saw his chance. Setting the words to Risk's tune, *Love Laughs at Locksmiths*, donning the costume of a Western riverman, and arming himself with a long "squirrel" rifle, he presented himself before the house. The

rivermen who filled the pit received him, it is related, with "a prolonged whoop, or howl, such as
Indians give when they are especially pleased."
And to these sturdy men the words of his song
made a strong appeal:

> We are a hardy, freeborn race,
>   Each man to fear a stranger;
> Whate'er the game, we join in chase,
>   Despising toil and danger;
> And if a daring foe annoys,
>   No matter what his force is,
> We'll show him that Kentucky boys
>   Are Alligator-horses.

The title "alligator-horse," of which Western
rivermen were very proud, carried with it a sugges-
tion of amphibious strength that made it both apt
and figuratively accurate. On all the American
rivers, east and west, a lusty crew, collected from
the waning Indian trade and the disbanded pioneer
armies, found work to its taste in poling the long
keel boats, "cordelling" the bulky barges — that
is, towing them by pulling on a line attached to
the shore — or steering the "broadhorns" or flatboats that transported the first heavy inland river
cargoes. Like longshoremen of all ages, the American riverman was as rough as the work which

calloused his hands and transformed his muscles into bands of tempered steel.   Like all men given to hard but intermittent labor, he employed his intervals of leisure in coarse and brutal recreation. Their roistering exploits, indeed, have made these rivermen almost better known at play than at work.   One of them, the notorious Mike Fink, known as "the Snag" on the Mississippi and as the "Snapping Turtle" on the Ohio, has left the record, not that he could load a keel boat in a certain length of time, or lift a barrel of whiskey with one arm, or that no tumultuous current had ever compelled him to back water, but that he could "out-run, out-hop, out-jump, throw down, drag out, and lick any man in the country," and that he was "a Salt River roarer."

Such men and the craft they handled were known on the Atlantic rivers, but it was on the Mississippi and its branches, especially the Ohio, that they played their most important part in the history of American inland commerce. Before the beginning of the nineteenth century wagons and Conestogas were bringing great loads of merchandise to such points on the headwaters as Brownsville, Pittsburgh, and Wheeling. As early as 1782, we are told, Jacob Yoder, a Pennsylvania German,

A FLATBOAT, SUCH AS WAS USED ON THE OHIO AND
MISSISSIPPI RIVERS, SOMETIMES CALLED
AN ARK, A VOITURE, OR A BROADHORN

Engraving, from a drawing made in 1796, in Victor Collot's
Voyage dans l'Amerique Septentrionale, published in Paris, 1826.
In the New York Public Library.

A FLATBOAT, SUCH AS IT WAS USED ON THE OHIO AND
MISSISSIPPI RIVERS, SOMETIMES CALLED
AN ARK, A VOITURE OR A BROADHORN

Engraving, from a drawing made in 1796, in Victor Collot's
Voyage dans l'Amerique Septentrionale, published in Paris, 1826.
In the New York Public Library

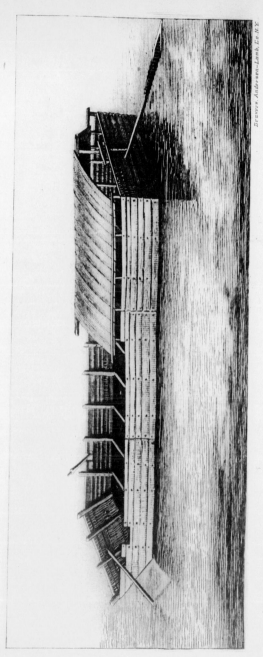

Gravure Anderson-Lamb, Co. N.Y.

set sail from the Monongahela country with the first flatboat to descend the Ohio and Mississippi. As the years passed, the number of such craft grew constantly larger. The custom of fixing the wide-spreading horns of cattle on the prow gave these boats the alternative name of "broadhorns," but no accurate classification can be made of the various kinds of craft engaged in this vast traffic. Everything that would float, from rough rafts to finished barges, was commandeered into service, and what was found unsuitable for the strenuous purposes of commercial transportation was palmed off whenever possible on unsuspecting emigrants *en route* to the lands of promise beyond.

Flour, salt, iron, cider and peach brandy were staple products of the Ohio country which the South desired. In return they shipped molasses, sugar, coffee, lead, and hides upon the few keel boats which crept upstream or the blundering barges which were propelled northward by means of oar, sail, and cordelle. It was not, however, until the nineteenth century that the young West was producing any considerable quantity of manu-factured goods. Though the town of Pittsburgh had been laid out in 1764, by the end of the Revolu-tion it was still little more than a collection of huts about a fort. A notable amount of local trade was carried on, but the expense of transportation was very high even after wagons began crossing the Alleghanies. For example, the cost from Philadelphia and Baltimore was given by Arthur Lee, a member of Congress, in 1784 as forty-five shillings a hundredweight, and a few months later it is quoted at sixpence a pound when Johann D. Schoph crossed the mountains in a chaise — a feat "which till now had been considered quite impossible." Opinions differed widely as to the future of the little town of five hundred inhabitants. The important product of the region at first was Monongahela flour which long held a high place in the New Orleans market. Coal was being mined as early as 1796 and was worth locally threepence halfpenny a bushel, though within seven years it was being sold at Philadelphia at thirty-seven and a half cents a bushel. The fur trade with the Illinois country grew less important as the century came to its close, but Maynard and Morrison, cooperating with Guy Bryan at Philadelphia, sent a barge laden with merchandise to Illinois annually between 1790 and 1796, which returned each season with a cargo of skins and furs. Pittsburgh was thus a distributing center of some importance;

but the fact that no drayman or warehouse was to be found in the town at this time is a significant commentary on the undeveloped state of its commerce and manufacture.

After Wayne's victory at the battle of the Fallen Timber in 1794 and the signing of the Treaty of Greenville in 1795, which ended the earlier Indian wars of the Old Northwest and opened for settlement the country beyond the Ohio, a great migration followed into Ohio, Indiana, and Kentucky, and the commercial activity of Pittsburgh rapidly increased. By 1800 a score of profitable industries had arisen, and by 1803 the first bar-iron foundry was, to quote the advertisement of its owner, "sufficiently upheld by the hand of the Almighty" to supply in part the demand for iron and castings. Glass factories were established, and ropewalks, sail lofts, boatyards, anchor smithies, and brickyards, were soon ready to supply the rapidly increasing demands of the infant cities and the countryside on the lower Ohio. When the new century arrived the Pittsburgh district had a population of upwards of two thousand.

One by one the other important centers of trade in the great valley beyond began to show evidences of life. Marietta, Ohio, founded in 1788 by

Revolutionary officers from New England, became the metropolis of the rich Muskingum River district, which was presently sending many flatboats southward.   Cincinnati was founded in the same year as Marietta, with the building of Fort Washington and the formal organization of Hamilton County.   The soil of the Miami country was as "mellow as an ash heap" and in the first four months of 1802 over four thousand barrels of flour were shipped southward to challenge the prestige of the Monongahela product.   Potters, brickmakers, gunsmiths, cotton and wool weavers, coopers, turners, wheelwrights, dyers, printers, and ropemakers were at work here within the next decade.   A brewery turned out five thousand barrels of beer and porter in 1811, and by the next year the pork-packing business was thoroughly established.

Louisville, the "Little Falls" of the West, was the entrepôt of the Blue Grass region.   It had been a place of some importance since Revolutionary days, for in seasons of low water the rapids in the Ohio at this point gave employment to scores of laborers who assisted the flatboatmen in hauling their cargoes around the obstruction which prevented the passage of the heavily loaded barges.

The town, which was incorporated in 1780, soon showed signs of commercial activity. It was the proud possessor of a drygoods house in 1783. The growth of its tobacco industry was rapid from the first. The warehouses were under government supervision and inspection as early as 1795, and innumerable flatboats were already bearing cargoes of bright leaf southward in the last decade of the century. The first brick house in Louisville was erected in 1789 with materials brought from Pittsburgh. Yankees soon established the "Hope Distillery"; and the manufacture of whiskey, which had long been a staple industry conducted by individuals, became an incorporated business of great promise in spite of objections raised against the "creation of gigantic reservoirs of this damning drink."

Thus, about the year 1800, the great industries of the young West were all established in the regions dominated by the growing cities of Pittsburgh, Cincinnati, and Louisville. But, since the combined population of these centers could not have been over three thousand in the year 1800, it is evident that the adjacent rural population and the people living in every neighboring creek and river valley were chiefly responsible for the large trade that already existed between this corner of the Mississippi basin and the South.

In this trade the riverman was the fundamental factor. Only by means of his brawn and his genius for navigation could these innumerable tons of flour, tobacco, and bacon have been kept from rotting on the shores. Yet the man himself remains a legend grotesque and mysterious, one of the shadowy figures of a time when history was being made too rapidly to be written. If we ask how he loaded his flatboat or barge, we are told that "one squint of his eye would blister a bull's heel." When we inquire how he found the channel amid the shifting bars and floating islands of that tortuous two-thousand-mile journey to New Orleans, we are informed that he was "the very infant that turned from his mother's breast and called out for a bottle of old rye." When we ask how he overcame the natural difficulties of trade — lack of commission houses, varying standards of money, want of systems of credit and low prices due to the glutting of the market when hundreds of flatboats arrived in the South simultaneously on the same freshet — we are informed that "Billy Earthquake is the geniwine, double-acting engine, and can out-run, out-swim, chaw more tobacco and spit less, drink more whiskey and keep soberer than any other man in these localities."

The reason for this lack of information is that our descriptions of flatboating and keel boating are written by travelers who, as is always the case, are interested in what is unusual, not in what is typical and commonplace. It is therefore only dimly, as through a mist, that we can see the two lines of polemen pass from the prow to the stern on the narrow running-board of a keel boat, lifting and setting their poles to the cry of steersman or captain. The struggle in a swift "riffle" or rapid is momentous. If the craft swerves, all is lost. Shoulders bend with savage strength; poles quiver under the tension; the captain's voice is raucous, and every other word is an oath; a pole breaks, and the next man, though half-dazed in the mortal crisis, does for a few moments the work of two. At last they reach the head of the rapid, and the boat floats out on the placid pool above, while the "alligator-horse" who had the mishap remarks to the scenery at large that he'd be "fly-blowed before sun-down to a certingty" if that were not the very pole with which he "pushed the broadhorn up Salt River where the snags were so thick that a fish couldn't swim without rubbing his scales off."

Audubon, the naturalist-merchant of the Mississippi, has left us a clear picture of the process by which these heavy tubs, loaded with forty or fifty tons of freight, were forced upstream against a swift current:

Wherever a point projected so as to render the course or bend below it of some magnitude, there was an eddy, the returning current of which was sometimes as strong as that of the middle of the great stream. The bargemen, therefore, rowed up pretty close under the bank and had merely to keep watch in the bow lest the boat should run against a planter or sawyer. But the boat has reached the point, and there the current is to all appearance of double strength and right against it. The men, who have rested a few minutes, are ordered to take their stations and lay hold of their oars, for the river must be crossed, it being seldom possible to double such a point and proceed along the same shore. The boat is crossing, its head slanting to the current, which is, however, too strong for the rowers, and when the other side of the river has been reached, it has drifted perhaps a quarter of a mile. The men are by this time exhausted and, as we shall suppose it to be 12 o'clock, fasten the boat to a tree on the shore. A small glass of whiskey is given to each, when they cook and eat their dinner and, after resting from their fatigue for an hour, recommence their labors. The boat is again seen slowly advancing against the stream. It has reached the lower end of a sandbar, along the edge of which it is propelled by means of long poles, if the bottom be hard. Two men, called bowsmen, remain at the prow to assist, in concert with the steersman, in managing the boat and keeping its head right against the current. The rest place themselves on the land side of the footway of the vessel, put one end of their poles on the ground and the other against their shoulders and push with all their might. As each of the men reaches the stern, he crosses to the other side, runs along it and comes again to the landward side of the bow, when he recommences operations. The barge in the meantime is ascending at a rate not exceeding one mile in the hour.

Trustworthy statistics as to the amount and character of the Western river trade have never been gathered. They are to be found, if anywhere, in the reports of the collectors of customs located at the various Western ports of entry and departure. Nothing indicates more definitely the hour when the West awoke to its first era of big business than the demand for the creation of "districts" and their respective ports, for by no other means could merchandise and produce be shipped legally to Spanish territory beyond or down the Mississippi or to English territory on the northern shores of the Great Lakes.

Louisville is as old a port of the United States as New York or Philadelphia, having been so created when our government was established in 1789, but oddly enough the first returns to the National Treasury (1798) are credited to the port of Palmyra, Tennessee, far inland on the Cumberland River. In 1799 the following Western towns were made ports of entry: Erie, Sandusky, Detroit, Mackinaw Island, and Columbia (Cincinnati). The first port on the Ohio to make returns was Fort Massac, Illinois, and it is from the collector at this point that we get our first hint as to the character and volume of Western river traffic. In the spring months of March, April, and May, 1800, cargoes to the value of £28,581, Pennsylvania currency, went down the Ohio. This included 22,714 barrels of flour, 1017 barrels of whiskey, 12,500 pounds of pork, 18,710 pounds of bacon, 75,814 pounds of cordage, 3650 yards of country linen, 700 bottles, and 700 barrels of potatoes. In the three autumn months of 1800, for instance, twenty-one boats ascended the Ohio by Fort Massac, with cargoes amounting to 36 hundredweight of lead and a few hides. Descending the river at the same time, flatboats and barges carried 245 hundredweight of drygoods valued at $32,550. When we compare these spring and fall records of commerce downstream we reach the natural conclusion that the bulk of the drygoods which went down in the fall of the year had been brought over the mountains during the summer. The fact that the Alleghany pack-horses and Conestogas were transporting freight to supply the Spanish towns on the Mississippi River in the first year of the nineteenth century seems proved beyond a doubt by these reports from Fort Massac.

The most interesting phase of this era is the connection between western trade and the politics of the Mississippi Valley which led up to the Louisiana Purchase. By the Treaty of San Lorenzo in 1795 Spain made New Orleans an open port, and in the next seven years the young West made the most of its opportunity. But before the new century was two years old the difficulties encountered were found to be serious. The lack of commission merchants, of methods of credit, of information as to the state of the market, all combined to handicap trade and to cause loss. Pittsburgh shippers figured their loss already at $60,000 a year. In consequence men began to look elsewhere, and an advocate of big business wrote in 1802: "The country has received a shock; let us immediately extend our views and direct our efforts to every foreign market."

One of the most remarkable plans for the capture of foreign trade to be found in the annals of American commerce originated almost simultaneously in the Muskingum and Monongahela regions. With a view to making the American West independent of the Spanish middlemen, it was proposed to build ocean-going vessels on the Ohio that should carry the produce of the interior down the Mississippi and thence abroad through the open port of New Orleans. The idea was typically Western in its arrogant originality and confident self-assertion. Two vessels were built: the brig *St. Clair*, of 110 tons, at Marietta, and the *Monongahela Farmer*, of 250 tons, at Elizabeth on the Monongahela. The former reached Cincinnati April 27, 1801; the latter, loaded with 750 barrels of flour, passed Pittsburgh on the 13th of May. Eventually, the *St. Clair* reached Havana and thus proved that Muskingum Valley black walnut, Ohio hemp, and Marietta carpenters, anchor smiths, and skippers could defy the grip of the Spaniard on the Mississippi. Other vessels followed these adventurers, and shipbuilding immediately became an important industry at Pittsburgh, Marietta, Cincinnati, and other points. The *Duane* of Pittsburgh was said by the Liverpool

Saturday Advertiser of July 9, 1803, to have been the "first vessel which ever came to Europe from the western waters of the United States." Probably the *Louisiana of Marietta* went as far afield as any of the one hundred odd ships built in these years on the Ohio. The official papers of her voyage in 1805, dated at New Orleans, Norfolk (Virginia), Liverpool, Messina, and Trieste at the head of the Adriatic, are preserved today in the Marietta College Library.

The growth of the shipbuilding industry necessitated a readjustment of the districts for the collection of customs. Columbia (Cincinnati) at first served the region of the upper Ohio; but in 1803 the district was divided and Marietta was made the port for the Pittsburgh-Portsmouth section of the river. In 1807 all the western districts were amalgamated, and Pittsburgh, Charleston (Wellsburg), Marietta, Cincinnati, Louisville, and Fort Massac were made ports of entry.

The Louisiana Purchase in 1803 gave a marked impulse to inland shipbuilding; but the embargo of 1807, which prohibited foreign trade, following so soon, killed the shipyards, which, for a few years, had been so busy. The great new industry of the Ohio Valley was ruined.

By this time the successful voyage of Fulton's steamboat, the *Clermont*, between New York and Albany, had demonstrated the possibilities of steam navigation. Not a few men saw in the novel craft the beginning of a new era in Western river traffic; but many doubted whether it was possible to construct a vessel powerful enough to make its way upstream against such sweeping currents as those of the Mississippi and the Ohio. Surely no one for a moment dreamed that in hardly more than a generation the Western rivers would carry a tonnage larger than that of the cities of the Atlantic seaboard combined and larger than that of Great Britain!

As early as 1805, two years before the trip of the *Clermont*, Captain Keever built a "steamboat" on the Ohio, and sent her down to New Orleans where her engine was to be installed. But it was not until 1811 that the *Orleans*, the first steamboat to ply the Western streams, was built at Pittsburgh, from which point she sailed for New Orleans in October of that year. The *Comet* and *Vesuvius* quickly followed, but all three entered the New Orleans-Natchez trade on the lower river and were never seen again at the headwaters. As yet the swift currents and flood tides of the great river had not been mastered. It is true that in 1815 the *Enterprise* had made two trips between New Orleans and Louisville, but this was in time of high water, when counter currents and backwaters had assisted her feeble engine. In 1816, however, Henry Shreve conceived the idea of raising the engine out of the hold and constructing an additional deck. The *Washington*, the first double-decker, was the result. The next year this steamboat made the round trip from Louisville to New Orleans and back in forty-one days. The doubters were now convinced.

For a little while the quaint and original riverman held on in the new age, only to disappear entirely when the colored roustabout became the deckhand of post-bellum days. The riverman as a type was unknown except on the larger rivers in the earlier years of water traffic. What an experience it would be today to rouse one of those remarkable individuals from his dreaming, as Davy Crockett did, with an oar, and hear him howl "Halloe stranger, who axed you to crack my lice?" — to tell him in his own lingo to "shut his mouth or he would get his teeth sunburnt" — to see him crook his neck and neigh like a stallion — to answer his challenge in kind with a flapping of arms and a cock's crow — to go to shore and have a scrimmage such as was never known on a gridiron — and then to resolve with Crockett, during a period of recuperation, that you would never "wake up a ring-tailed roarer with an oar again."

The riverman, his art, his language, his traffic, seem to belong to days as distant as those of which Homer sang.

CHAPTER VI

THE PASSING SHOW OF 1800

FOREIGN travelers who have come to the United States have always proved of great interest to Americans. From Brissot to Arnold Bennett, while in the country they have been fed and clothed and transported wheresoever they would go — at the highest prevailing prices. And after they have left, the records of their sojourn that these travelers have published have made interesting reading for Americans all over the land. Some of these trans-Atlantic visitors have been jaundiced, disgruntled, and contemptuous; others have shown themselves of an open nature, discreet, conscientious, and fair-minded.

One of the most amiable and clear-headed of such foreign guests was Francis Baily, later in life president of the Royal Astronomical Society of Great Britain, but at the time of his American tour a young man of twenty-two. His journey in

1796–97 gave him a wide experience of stage, flat-boat, and pack-horse travel, and his genial disposi-tion, his observant eye, and his discriminating criticism, together with his comments on the com-mercial features of the towns and regions he visited, make his record particularly interesting and valu-able to the historian.[1] Using Baily's journal as a guide, therefore, one can today journey with him across the country and note the passing show as he saw it in this transitional period.

Landing at Norfolk, Virginia, Baily was imme-diately introduced to an American tavern. Like most travelers, he was surprised to find that Ameri-can taverns were "boarding-places," frequented by crowds of "young, able-bodied men who seemed to be as perfectly at leisure as the loungers of an-cient Europe." In those days of few newspapers, the tavern everywhere in America was the center of information; in fact, it was a common practice for travelers in the interior, after signing their names in the register, to add on the same page any news of local interest which they brought with them. The tavern habitués, Baily remarks, did not sit and drink after meals but "wasted" their

[1] *Journal of a Tour in Unsettled Parts of North America in 1796 and 1797* by the late Francis Baily (London, 1856).

time at billiards and cards. The passion for billiards was notorious, and taverns in the most out-of-the-way places, though they lacked the most ordinary conveniences, were nevertheless provided with billiard tables. This custom seems to have been especially true in the South; and it is significant that the first taxes in Tennessee levied before the beginning of the nineteenth century were the poll tax and taxes on billiard tables and studhorses!

From Norfolk Baily passed northward to Baltimore, paying a fare of ten dollars, and from there he went on to Philadelphia, paying six dollars more. On the way his stagecoach stuck fast in a bog and the passengers were compelled to leave it until the next morning. This sixty-mile road out of Baltimore was evidently one of the worst in the East. Ten years prior to this date, Brissot, a keen French journalist, mentions the great ruts in its heavy clay soil, the overturned trees which blocked the way, and the unexampled skilfulness of the stage drivers. All travelers in America, though differing on almost every other subject, invariably praise the ability of these sturdy, weather-beaten American drivers, their kindness to their horses, and their attention to their passengers. Harriet Martineau stated that, in her experience, American drivers as a class were marked by the merciful temper which accompanies genius, and their perfection in their art, their fertility of resource, and the gentleness with which they treated female fears and fretfulness, were exemplary.

In the City of Brotherly Love Baily notes the geniality of the people, who by many travelers are called aristocratic, and comments on Quaker opposition to the theater and the inconsequence of the Peale Museum, which travelers a generation later highly praise. Proceeding to New York at a cost of six dollars, he is struck by the uncouthness of the public buildings, churches excepted, the widespread passion for music, dancing, and the theater, the craze for sleighing, and the promise which the harbor gave of becoming the finest in America. Not a few travelers in this early period gave expression to their belief in the future greatness of New York City. These prophecies, taken in connection with the investment of eight millions of dollars which New Yorkers made in toll-roads in the first seven years of this new century, incline one to believe that the influence of the Erie Canal as a factor in the development of the city may have been unduly emphasized, great though it was.

From New York Baily returned to Baltimore

and went on to Washington. The records of all travelers to the site of the new national capital give much the same picture of the countryside. It was a land worn out by tobacco culture and variously described as "dried up," "run down," and "hung out to dry." Even George Washington, at Mount Vernon, was giving up tobacco culture and was attempting new crops by a system of rotation. Cotton was being grown in Maryland, but little care was given to its culture and manufacture. Tobacco was graded in Virginia in accordance with the rigidity of its inspection at Hanover Court House, Pittsburgh, Richmond, and Cabin-Point: leaf worth sixteen shillings at Richmond was worth twenty-one at Hanover Court House; if it was refused at all places, it was smuggled to the West Indies or consumed in the country. Meadows were rapidly taking the place of tobacco-fields, for the planters preferred to clear new land rather than to enrich the old.

At Washington Baily found that lots to the value of $278,000 had been sold, although only one-half of the proposed city had been "cleared." It was to be forty years ere travelers could speak respectfully of what is now the beautiful city of Washington. In these earlier days, the streets were mudholes divided by vacant fields and "beautified by trees, swamps, and cows."

Departing for the West by way of Frederick, Baily, like all travelers, was intensely interested upon entering the rich limestone region which stretched from Pennsylvania far down into Virginia. It was occupied in part by the Pennsylvania Dutch and was so famous for its rich milk that it was called by many travelers the "Bonnyclabber Country." Most Englishmen were delighted with this region because they found here the good old English breed of horses, that is, the English hunter developed into a stout coach-horse. Of native breeds, Baily found animals of all degrees of strength and size down to hackneys of fourteen hands, as well as the "vile dog-horses," or pack-horses, whose faithful service to the frontier could in no wise be appreciated by a foreigner.

This region of Pennsylvania was as noted for its wagons as for its horses. It was this wheat-bearing belt that made the common freight-wagon in its colors of red and blue a national institution. It was in this region of rich, well-watered land that the maple tree gained its reputation. Men even prophesied that its delightful sap would prove a cure for slavery, for, if one family could make fifteen hundred pounds of maple sugar in a season, eighty thousand families could, at the same rate, equal the output of cane sugar each year from Santo Domingo!

The traveler at the beginning of the century noticed a change in the temper of the people as well as a change in the soil when the Bonnyclabber Country was reached. The time-serving attitude of the good people of the East now gave place to a "consciousness of independence" due, Baily remarks, to the fact that each man was self-sufficient and passed his life "without regard to the smiles and frowns of men in power." This spirit was handsomely illustrated in the case of one burly Westerner who was "churched" for fighting. Showing a surly attitude to the deacon-judges who sat on his case, he was threatened with civil prosecution and imprisonment. "I don't want freedom," he is said to have replied, bitterly; "I don't even want to live if I can't knock down a man who calls me a liar."

Pushing on westward by way of historic Sideling Hill and Bedford to Statlers, Baily found here a prosperous millstone quarry, which sold its stones at from fifteen to thirty dollars a pair. Twelve years earlier Washington had prophesied that the

Alleghanies would soon be furnishing millstones equal to the best English burr. As he crossed the mountains Baily found that taverns charged the following schedule: breakfast, eighteen pence; dinner and supper from two shillings to two shillings and sixpence each. Traversing Laurel Hill, he reached Pittsburgh just at the time when it was awakening to activity as the trading center of the West.

In order to descend the Ohio, Baily obtained a flatboat, thirty-six feet long and twelve feet broad, which drew eighteen inches of water and was of ten tons burden. On the way downstream, Charleston and Wheeling were the principal settlements which Baily first noted. Ebenezer Zane, the founder of Wheeling, had just opened across Ohio the famous landward route from the Monongahela country to Kentucky, which it entered at Limestone, the present Maysville. This famous road, passing through Zanesville, Lancaster, and Chillicothe, though at that time safe only for men in parties, was a common route to and from Kentucky.

On such inland pathways as this, early travelers came to take for granted a hospitality not to be found on more frequented thoroughfares. In this hospitality, roughness and good will, cleanliness and filth, attempts to ape the style of Eastern towns and habits of the most primitive kind, were singularly blended. In one instance, the traveler might be cordially assigned by the landlord to a good position in "the first rush for a chance at the head of the table"; at the next stopping place he might be coldly turned away because the proprietor "had the gout" and his wife the "delicate blue-devils"; farther on, where "soap was unknown, nothing clean but birds, nothing industrious but pigs, and nothing happy but squirrels," Daniel Boone's daughter might be seen in high-heeled shoes, attended by white servants whose wages were a dollar a week, skirting muddy roads under a ten-dollar bonnet and a six-dollar parasol. Or, he might emerge from a lonely forest in Ohio or Indiana and come suddenly upon a party of neighbors at a dreary tavern, enjoying a corn shucking or a harvest home. Immediately dubbed "Doctor," "Squire," or "Colonel" by the hospitable merrymakers, the passer-by would be informed that he "should drink and lack no good thing." After he had retired, as likely as not his quarters would be invaded at one or two o'clock in the morning by the uproarious company, and the best refreshment of the house would be forced upon him with a hilarity "created by omnipotent whiskey." Sometimes, however, the traveler would encounter pitiful instances of loneliness in the wide-spreading forests. One man in passing a certain isolated cabin was implored by the woman who inhabited it to rest awhile and talk, since she was, she confessed, completely overwhelmed by "the lone!"

Every traveler has remarked upon the yellow pallor of the first inhabitants of the western forests and doubtless correctly attributed this sickly appearance to the effects of malaria and miasma. The psychic influences of the forest wilderness also weighed heavily upon the spirits of the settlers, although, as Baily notes, it was the newcomers who felt the depression to an exaggerated degree. As he says:

It is a feeling of confinement, which begins to damp the spirits, from this complete exclusion of distant objects. To travel day after day, among trees of a hundred feet high, is oppressive to a degree which those cannot conceive who have not experienced it; and it must depress the spirits of the solitary settler to pass years in this state. His visible horizon extends no farther than the tops of the trees which bound his plantation — perhaps five hundred yards. Upwards he sees the sun, and sky, and stars, but around him an

eternal forest, from which he can never hope to emerge:
— not so in a thickly settled district; he cannot there
enjoy any freedom of prospect, yet there is variety,
and some scope for the imprisoned vision. In a hilly
country a little more range of view may occasionally be obtained; and a river is a stream of light as
well as of water, which feasts the eye with a delight
inconceivable to the inhabitants of open countries.

In direct contradiction to this longing for society was the passion which the first generation of
pioneers had for the wilderness. When the population of one settlement became too thick, they
were seized by an irresistible impulse to "follow
the migration," as the expression went. The easy
independence of the first hunter-agriculturalist
was upset by the advance of immigration. His
range was curtailed, his freedom limited. His
very breath seems to have become difficult. So
he sold out at a phenomenal profit, put out his fire,
shouldered his gun, called his dog, and set off again
in search of the solitude he craved.

Severe winter weather overtook Baily as he descended the Ohio River, until below Grave Creek
floating ice wrecked his boat and drove him ashore.
Here in the primeval forest, far from "Merrie
England," Baily spent the Christmas of 1796 in
building a new flatboat. This task completed, he

resumed his journey. Passing Marietta, where the bad condition of the winter roads prevented a visit to a famous Indian mound, he reached Limestone. In due time he sighted Columbia, the metropolis of the Miami country. According to Baily, the sale of European goods in this part of the Ohio Valley netted the importers a hundred per cent. Prices varied with the ease of navigation. When ice blocked the Ohio the price of flour went up until it was eight dollars a barrel; whiskey was a dollar a gallon; potatoes, a dollar a bushel; and bacon, twelve cents a pound. At these prices, the total produce which went by Fort Massac in the early months of 1800 would have been worth on the Ohio River upwards of two hundred thousand dollars! In the preceding summer Baily quoted flour at Norfolk as selling at sixty-three shillings a barrel of 196 pounds, or double the price it was bringing on the ice-gorged Ohio. It is by such comparisons that we get some inkling of the value of western produce and of the rates in western trade.

After a short stay at Cincinnati, Baily set out for the South on an "Orleans boat" loaded with four hundred barrels of flour. At the mouth of Pigeon Creek he noted the famous path to "Post

St. Vincent's" (Vincennes), over which he saw
emigrants driving cattle to that ancient town on
the Wabash. At Fort Massac he met Captain
Zebulon M. Pike, whose tact in dealing with in-
toxicated Indians he commended. At New Madrid Baily made a stay of some days. This settlement, consisting of some two hundred and fifty
houses, was in the possession of Spain. It was
within the province of Louisiana, soon to be ceded
to Napoleon. New Orleans supplied this district
with merchandise, but smuggling from the United
States was connived at by the Spanish officials.

From New Madrid Baily proceeded to Natchez,
which then contained about eighty-five houses.
The town did not boast a tavern, but, as was true
of other places in the interior, this lack was made
up for by the hospitality of its inhabitants. Rice
and tobacco were being grown, Baily notes, and
Georgian cotton was being raised in the neighborhood. Several jennies were already at work, and
their owners received a royalty of one-eighth of
the product. The cotton was sent to New Orleans,
where it usually sold for twenty dollars a hundred
weight. From Natchez to New Orleans the charge
for transportation by flatboat was a dollar and a
half a bag. The bags contained from one hundred

and fifty to two hundred and fifty pounds, and each flatboat carried about two hundred and fifty bags. Baily adds two items to the story of the development of the mechanical operation of watercraft. He tells us that in the fall of 1796 a party of "Dutchmen," in the Pittsburgh region, fashioned a boat with side paddle wheels which were turned by a treadmill worked by eight horses under the deck. This strange boat, which passed Baily when he was wrecked on the Ohio near Grave Creek, appeared "to go with prodigious swiftness." Baily does not state how much business the boat did on its downward trip to New Orleans but contents himself with remarking that the owners expected the return trip to prove very profitable. When he met the boat on its upward voyage at Natchez, it had covered three hundred miles in six days. It was, however, not loaded, "so little occasion was there for a vessel of this kind." As this run between New Orleans and Natchez came to be one of the most profitable in the United States in the early days of steamboating, less than fifteen years later, the experience of these "Flying Dutchmen" affords a very pretty proof that something more than a means of transportation is needed to create commerce. The owners abandoned their craft at Natchez in disgust and returned home across country, wiser and poorer.

Baily also noted that a Dr. Waters of New Madrid built a schooner "some few years since" at the head of the Ohio and navigated it down the Ohio and Mississippi and around to Philadelphia, "where it is now employed in the commerce of the United States." It is thus apparent, solely from this traveler's record, that an ocean-going vessel and a side-paddle-wheel boat had been seen on the Western Waters of the United States at least four years before the nineteenth century arrived.

Baily finally reached New Orleans. The city then contained about a thousand houses and was not only the market for the produce of the river plantations but also the center of an extensive Indian trade. The goods for this trade were packed in little barrels which were carried into the interior on pack-horses, three barrels to a horse. The traders traveled for hundreds of miles through the woods, bartering with the Indians on the way and receiving, in exchange for their goods, bear and deer skins, beaver furs, and wild ponies which had been caught by lariat in the neighboring Apalousa country.

Baily had intended to return to New York by

sea, but on his arrival at New Orleans he was un-
able to find a ship sailing to New York. He therefore decided to proceed northward by way of the
long and dangerous Natchez Trace and the Tennessee Path. Though few Europeans had made
this laborious journey before 1800, the Natchez
Trace had been for many years the land route of
thousands of returning rivermen who had descended the Mississippi in flatboat and barge. In
practically all cases these men carried with them
the proceeds of their investment, and, as on every
thoroughfare in the world traveled by those returning from market, so here, too, highwaymen
and desperadoes, red and white, built their lairs
and lay in wait. Some of the most revolting crimes
of the American frontier were committed on these
northward pathways and their branches.

Joining a party bound for Natchez, a hundred
and fifty miles distant overland, Baily proceeded
to Lake Pontchartrain and thence "north by west
through the woods," by way of the ford of the
Tangipahoa, Cooper's Plantation, Tickfaw River,
Amite River, and the "Hurricane" (the path of a
tornado) to the beginning of the Apalousa country.
This tangled region of stunted growth was reputed
to be seven miles in width from "shore to shore"

MODEL OF JOHN FITCH'S STEAMBOAT, 1797

In the collection of the New York Historical Society.

MODEL OF JOHN FITCH'S STEAMBOAT, 1787

In the collection of the New York Historical Society

Bravura, Andersen - Lamb. Co. N. Y.

and three hundred miles in length. It took the party half a day to reach the opposite "shore," and they had to quench their thirst on the way with dew.

At Natchez, Baily organized a party which included the five "Dutchmen" whose horse boat had proved a failure. For their twenty-one days' journey to Nashville the party laid in the following provisions: 15 pounds of biscuit, 6 pounds of flour, 12 pounds of bacon, 10 pounds of dried beef, 3 pounds of rice, 1½ pounds of coffee, 4 pounds of sugar, and a quantity of pounded corn, such as the Indians used on all their journeys. After celebrating the Fourth of July, 1797, with "all the inhabitants who were hostile to the Spanish Government," and bribing the baker at the Spanish fort to bake them a quarter of a hundredweight of bread, the party started on their northward journey.

They reached without incident the famous Grindstone Ford of Bayou Pierre, where crayfishes had destroyed a pioneer dam. Beyond, at the forks of the path where the Choctaw Trail bore off to the east the party pursued the alternate Chickasaw Trail by Indian guidance, and soon noted the change in the character of the soil from black loam to sandy gravel, which indicated that

7

they had reached the Piedmont region. Indian marauders stole one horse from the camp, and three of the party fell ill. The others, pressed for food, were compelled to leave the sick men in an improvised camp and to hasten on, promising to send to their aid the first Indian they should meet "who understood herbs." After appalling hardships, they crossed the Tennessee and entered the Nashville country, where the roads were good enough for coaches, for they met two on the way. Thence Baily proceeded to Knoxville, seeing, as he went, droves of cattle bound for the settlements of west Tennessee. With his arrival at Knoxville, his journal ends abruptly; but from other sources we learn that he sailed from New York on his return to England in January, 1798. His interesting record, however, remained unpublished until after his death in 1844.

Not only to Francis Baily but to scores of other travelers, even those of unfriendly eyes, do modern readers owe a debt of gratitude. These men have preserved a multitude of pictures and a wealth of data which would otherwise have been lost. The men of America in those days were writing the story of their deeds not on parchment or paper but on the virgin soil of the wilderness. But though the stage driver, the tavern keeper, and the burly riverman left no description of the life of their highways and their commerce, these visitors from other lands have bequeathed to us their thousands of pages full of the enterprising life of these pioneer days in the history of American commerce.

CHAPTER VII

THE BIRTH OF THE STEAMBOAT

THE crowds who welcomed the successive stages in the development of American transportation were much alike in essentials — they were all optimistic, self-congratulatory, irrepressible in their enthusiasm, and undaunted in their outlook. Dickens, perhaps, did not miss the truth widely when, in speaking of stage driving, he said that the cry of "Go Ahead!" in America and of "All Right!" in England were typical of the civilizations of the two countries. Right or wrong, "Go Ahead!" has always been the underlying passion of all men interested in the development of commerce and transportation in these United States.

During the era of river improvement already described, men of imagination were fascinated with the idea of propelling boats by mechanical means. Even when Washington fared westward in 1784, he met at Bath, Virginia, one of these early experimenters, James Rumsey, who haled him forthwith to a neighboring meadow to watch a secret trial of a boat moved by means of machinery which worked setting-poles similar to the iron-shod poles used by the rivermen to propel their boats upstream. "The model," wrote Washington, "and its operation upon the water, which had been made to run pretty swift, not only convinced me of what I before thought next to, if not quite impracticable, but that it might be to the greatest possible utility in inland navigation." Later he mentions the "discovery" as one of those "circumstances which have combined to render the present epoch favorable above all others for securing a large portion of the produce of the western settlements, and of the fur and peltry of the Lakes, also."

From that day forward, scarcely a week passed without some new development in the long and difficult struggle to improve the means of navigation. Among the scores of men who engaged in this engrossing but discouraging work, there is one whom the world is coming to honor more highly than in previous years — John Fitch, of Connecticut, Pennsylvania, and Kentucky. As early as August, 1785, Fitch launched on a rivulet in Bucks

County, Pennsylvania, a boat propelled by an engine which moved an endless chain to which little paddles were attached. The next year, Fitch's second boat, operated by twelve paddles, six on a side — an arrangement suggesting the "side-wheeler" of the future — successfully plied the Delaware off "Conjuror's Point," as the scene of Fitch's labors was dubbed in whimsical amusement and derision. In 1787 Rumsey, encouraged by Franklin, fashioned a boat propelled by a stream of water taken in at the prow and ejected at the stern. In 1788 Fitch's third boat traversed the distance from Philadelphia to Burlington on numerous occasions and ran as a regular packet in 1790, covering over a thousand miles. In this model Fitch shifted the paddles from the sides to the rear, thus anticipating in principle the modern stern-wheeler.

It was doubtless Fitch's experiments in 1785 that led to the first plan in America to operate a land vehicle by steam. Oliver Evans, a neighbor and acquaintance of Fitch's, petitioned the Pennsylvania Legislature in 1786 for the right of operating wagons propelled by steam on the highways of that State. This petition was derisively rejected; but a similar one made to the Legislature of Maryland was granted on the ground that such action could hurt nobody. Evans in 1802 took fiery revenge on the scoffers by actually running his little five-horse-power carriage through Philadelphia. The rate of speed, however, was so slow that the idea of moving vehicles by steam was still considered useless for practical purposes. Eight years later, Evans offered to wager $3000 that, on a level road, he could make a carriage driven by steam equal the speed of the swiftest horse, but he found no response. In 1812 he asserted that he was willing to wager that he could drive a steam carriage on level rails at a rate of fifteen miles an hour. Evans thus anticipated the belief of Stephenson that steam-driven vehicles would travel best on railed tracks.

In the development of the steamboat almost all earlier means of propulsion, natural and artificial, were used as models by the inventors. The fins of fishes, the webbed feet of amphibious birds, the paddles of the Indian, and the poles and oars of the riverman, were all imitated by the patient inventors struggling with the problem. Rumsey's first effort was a copy of the old setting-pole idea. Fitch's model of 1785 had side paddle wheels operated by an endless chain. Fitch's second and third models were practically paddle-wheel models, one having the paddles at the side and the other at the stern. Ormsbee of Connecticut made a model, in 1792, on the plan of a duck's foot. Morey made what may be called the first real stern-wheeler in 1794. Two years later Fitch ran a veritable screw propeller on Collect Pond near New York City. Although General Benjamin Tupper of Massachusetts had been fashioning devices of this character eight years previously, Fitch was the first to apply the idea effectively. In 1798 he evolved the strange, amphibious creation known as his "model of 1798," which has never been adequately explained. It was a steamboat on iron wheels provided with flanges, as though it was intended to be run on submerged tracks. What may have been the idea of its inventor, living out his last gloomy days in Kentucky, may never be known; but it is possible to see in this anomalous machine an anticipation of the locomotive not approached by any other American of the time. Thus, prior to 1800 almost every type of mechanism for the propulsion of steamboats had been suggested and tried; and in 1804, Stevens's twin-screw propeller completed the list.

It is not alone Fitch's development of the devices of the endless chain, paddle wheel, and screw propeller and of his puzzling earth-and-water creature that gives luster to his name. His prophetic insight into the future national importance of the steamboat and his conception, as an inventor, of his moral obligations to the people at large were as original and striking in the science of that age as were his models.

The early years of the national life of the United States were the golden age of monopoly. Every colony, as a matter of course, had granted to certain men special privileges, and, as has already been pointed out, the questions of monopolies and combinations in restraint of trade had arisen even so early as the beginning of the eighteenth century. Interwoven inextricably with these problems was the whole problem of colonial rivalry, which in its later form developed into an insistence on state rights. Every improvement in the means of transportation, every development of natural resources, every new invention was inevitably considered from the standpoint of sectional interests and with a view to its monopolistic possibilities. This was particularly true in the case of the steamboat, because of its limitation to rivers and bays which could be specifically enumerated and defined. For instance, Washington in 1784 attests the fact that Rumsey operated his mechanical boat at Bath in secret "until he saw the effect of an application he was about to make to the Assembly of this State, for a reward." The application was successful, and Rumsey was awarded a monopoly in Virginia waters for ten years.

Fitch, on the other hand, when he applied to Congress in 1785, desired merely to obtain official encouragement and intended to allow his invention to be used by all comers. Meeting only with rebuff, he realized that his only hope of organizing a company that could provide working capital lay in securing monopolistic privileges. In 1786 he accordingly applied to the individual States and secured the sole right to operate steamboats on the waterways of New Jersey, Delaware, New York, Pennsylvania, and Virginia. How different would have been the story of the steamboat if Congress had accepted Fitch at his word and created a precedent against monopolistic rights on American rivers!

Fitch, in addition to the high purpose of devoting his new invention to the good of the nation without personal considerations, must be credited with perceiving at the very beginning the peculiar importance of the steamboat to the American West.

His original application to Congress in 1785 opened: "The subscriber begs leave to lay at the feet of Congress, an attempt he has made to facilitate the internal Navigation of the United States, adapted especially to the Waters of the Mississippi." At another time with prophetic vision he wrote: "The Grand and Principle object must be on the Atlantick, which would soon overspread the wild forests of America with people, and make us the most oppulent Empire on Earth. Pardon me, generous public, for suggesting ideas that cannot be dijested at this day."

Foremost in exhibiting high civic and patriotic motives, Fitch was also foremost in appreciating the importance of the steamboat in the expansion of American trade. This significance was also clearly perceived by his brilliant successor, Robert Fulton. That the West and its commerce were always predominant in Fulton's great schemes is proved by words which he addressed in 1803 to James Monroe, American Ambassador to Great Britain: "You have perhaps heard of the success of my experiments for navigating boats by steam engines and you will feel the importance of establishing such boats on the Mississippi and other rivers of the United States as soon as possible."

Robert Fulton had been interested in steamboats for a period not definitely known, possibly since his sojourn in Philadelphia in the days of Fitch's early efforts. That he profited by the other inventor's efforts at the time, however, is not suggested by any of his biographers. He subsequently went to London and gave himself up to the study and practice of engineering. There he later met James Rumsey, who came to England in 1788, and by him no doubt was informed, if he was not already aware, of the experiments and models of Rumsey and Fitch. He obtained the loan of Fitch's plans and drawings and made his own trial of various existing devices, such as oars, paddles, duck's feet, and Fitch's endless chain with "resisting-boards" attached. Meanwhile Fulton was also devoting his attention to problems of canal construction and to the development of submarine boats and submarine explosives. He was engaged in these researches in France in 1801 when the new American minister, Robert R. Livingston, arrived, and the two men soon formed a friendship destined to have a vital and enduring influence upon the development of steam navigation on the inland waterways of America.

Livingston already had no little experience in

the same field of invention as Fulton. In 1798 he had obtained, for a period of twenty years, the right to operate steamboats on all the waters of the State of New York, a monopoly which had just lapsed owing to the death of Fitch. In the same year Livingston had built a steamboat which had made three miles an hour on the Hudson. He had experimented with most of the models then in existence — upright paddles at the side, endless-chain paddles, and stern paddle wheels. Fulton was soon inspired to resume his efforts by Livingston's account of his own experiments and of recent advances in England, where a steamboat had navigated the Thames in 1801 and a year later the famous stern-wheeler *Charlotte Dundas* had towed boats of 140 tons' burden on the Forth and Clyde Canal at the rate of five miles an hour. In this same year Fulton and Livingston made successful experiments on the Seine.

It is fortunate that, in one particular, Livingston's influence did not prevail with Fulton, for the American Minister was distinctly prejudiced against paddle wheels. Although Livingston had previously ridden as a passenger on Morey's stern-wheeler at the rate of five miles an hour, yet he had turned a deaf ear when his partner in experimentation, Nicholas J. Roosevelt, had insisted strongly on "throwing wheels over the sides." At the beginning, Fulton himself was inclined to agree with Livingston in this respect; but, probably late in 1803, he began to investigate more carefully the possibilities of the paddle wheel as used twice in America by Morey and by four or five experimenters in Europe. In 1804 an eight-mile trip which Fulton made on the *Charlotte Dundas* in an hour and twenty minutes established his faith in the undeniable superiority of two fundamental factors of early navigation — paddle wheels and British engines. Fulton's splendid fame rests, and rightly so, on his perception of the fact that no mere ingenuity of design could counterbalance weakness, uncertainty, and inefficiency in the mechanism which was intended to make a steamboat run and keep running. As early as November, 1803, Fulton had written to Boulton and Watt of Birmingham that he had "not confidence in any other engines" than theirs and that he was seeking a means of getting one of those engines to America. "I cannot establish the boat without the engine," he now emphatically wrote to James Monroe, then Ambassador to the Court of St. James. "The question then is shall we or shall we not have such boats."

But there were difficulties in the way. Though England forbade the exportation of engines, Fulton knew that, in numerous instances, this rule had not been enforced, and he had hopes of success. "The British Government," Fulton wrote Monroe, "must have little friendship or even civility toward America, if they refuse such a request." Before the steamboat which Fulton and Livingston proposed to build in America could be operated there was another obstacle to be surmounted. The rights of steam navigation of New York waters which Livingston had obtained on the death of Fitch in 1798 had lapsed because of his failure to run a steamboat at the rate of four miles an hour, which was one provision of the grant. In April, 1803, the grant was renewed to Livingston, Roosevelt, and Fulton jointly for another period of twenty years, and the date when the boat was to make the required four miles an hour was extended finally to 1807.

Any one who is inclined to criticize the Livingston-Roosevelt-Fulton monopoly which now came into existence should remember that the previous state grants formed a precedent of no slight moment. The whole proceeding was in perfect accord with the spirit of the times, for it was an era of speculation and monopoly ushered in by the toll-road and turnpike organizations, when probably no less than two hundred companies were formed. It was young America showing itself in an unmistakable manner — "conceived in liberty" and starting on the long road to learn that obedience to law and respect for public rights constitute true liberty. Finally, it must be pointed out that Fulton, like his famous predecessor, Fitch, was impelled by motives far higher than the love of personal gain. "I consider them [steamboats] of such infinite use in America," he wrote Monroe, "that I should feel a culpable neglect toward my country if I relaxed for a moment in pursuing every necessary measure for carrying it into effect." And later, when repeating his argument, he says: "I plead this not for myself alone but for our country."

It is now evident why the alliance of Fulton with Livingston was of such epoch-making importance, for, although it may have in some brief measure delayed Fulton's adoption of paddle wheels, it gave him an entry to the waters of New York. Livingston and Fulton thus supplemented each other; Livingston possessed a monopoly and Fulton a correct estimate of the value of paddle wheels

ROBERT FULTON'S FIRST STEAMBOAT

Drawing by Richard Varick DeWitt. In the collection of the New York Historical Society. The inscription on the drawing states that the upper picture represents the *Clermont* as she was used for a packet-boat in 1807, drawn from personal recollection and description of persons who traveled in the boat. It was about 100 feet long, propelled by a cross-head bell-crank engine of 24 horse-power, made by Watt and Boulton. During the next winter the vessel was enlarged to about 150 feet in length and 18 feet in width, and the wheels were placed within the hull. The original engines were retained. It was named the *North River of Clermont*, and its appearance is shown in the lower picture. Accompanying the inscription is the following certification:

"I, Riley Bartholomew, for some time an officer of the Steamboat North River of Clermont, certify the above to be a correct representation of that vessel.

"RILEY BARTHOLOMEW."

"Albany, September, 1858."

ROBERT FULTON'S FIRST STEAMBOAT

Drawing by Richard Varick DeWitt. In the collection of the *New York Historical Society*. The inscription on the drawing states that the upper picture represents the *Clermont* as she was used for a packet-boat in 1807, drawn from personal recollection and description of persons who traveled in the boat. It was about 100 feet long, propelled by a cross-head bell-crank engine of 24 horse-power, made by Watt and Boulton. During the next winter the vessel was enlarged to about 150 feet in length and 18 feet in width, and the wheels were placed within the hull. The original engines were retained. It was named the *North River* of *Clermont*, and its appearance is shown in the lower picture. Accompanying the inscription is the following certification:

"I, Riley Bartholomew, for some time an officer of the Steamboat *North River* of *Clermont*, certify the above to be a correct representation of that vessel.

"Riley Bartholomew.

"Albany, September, 1858."

CLERMONT.

Gravure, Anderson-Lamb Co. N.Y.

and, secondly, of Boulton and Watt engines. It was a rare combination destined to crown with success a long period of effort and discouragement in the history of navigation.

After considerable delay and difficulty, the two Americans obtained permission to export the necessary engine from Great Britain and shipped it to New York, whither Fulton himself proceeded to construct his steamboat. The hull was built by Charles Brown, a New York shipbuilder, and the Boulton and Watt machinery, set in masonry, was finally installed.

The voyage to Albany, against a stiff wind, occupied thirty-two hours; the return trip was made in thirty. H. Freeland, one of the spectators who stood on the banks of the Hudson when the boat made its maiden voyage in 1807, gives the following description:

Some imagined it to be a sea-monster whilst others did not hesitate to express their belief that it was a sign of the approaching judgment. What seemed strange in the vessel was the substitution of lofty and straight smoke-pipes, rising from the deck, instead of the gracefully tapered masts . . . and, in place of the spars and rigging, the curious play of the walking-beam and pistons, and the slow turning and splashing of the huge and naked paddle-wheels, met the

8

astonished gaze. The dense clouds of smoke, as they rose, wave upon wave, added still more to the wonderment of the rustics. . . . On her return trip the curiosity she excited was scarcely less intense . . . fishermen became terrified, and rode homewards, and they saw nothing but destruction devastating their fishing grounds, whilst the wreaths of black vapor and rushing noise of the paddle-wheels, foaming with the stirred-up water, produced great excitement. . . .

With the launching of the *Clermont* on the Hudson a new era in American history began. How quick with life it was many of the preceding pages bear testimony. The infatuation of the public for building toll and turnpike roads was now at its height. Only a few years before, a comprehensive scheme of internal improvements had been outlined by Jefferson's Secretary of the Treasury, Albert Gallatin. When a boy, it is said, he had lain on the floor of a surveyor's cabin on the western slopes of the Alleghanies and had heard Washington describe to a rough crowd of Westerners his plan to unite the Great Lakes with the Potomac in one mighty chain of inland commerce. Jefferson's Administration was now about to devote the surplus in the Treasury to the construction of national highways and canals. The Cumberland Road, to be built across the Alleghanies

by the War Department, was authorized by the
President in the same year in which the *Clermont*
made her first trip; and Jesse Hawley, at his table
in a little room in a Pittsburgh boarding house,
was even now penning in a series of articles, published in the Pittsburgh *Commonwealth*, beginning
in January, 1807, the first clear challenge to the
Empire State to connect the Hudson and Lake
Erie by a canal.   Thus the two next steps in the
history of inland commerce in America were ready
to be taken.

CHAPTER VIII

THE CONQUEST OF THE ALLEGHANIES

THE two great thoroughfares of American commerce in the first half of the nineteenth century were the Cumberland Road and the Erie Canal. The first generation of the new century witnessed the great burst of population into the West which at once gave Ohio, Indiana, Illinois, Michigan, and Wisconsin a place of national importance which they have never relinquished. So far as pathways of commerce contributed to the creation of this veritable new republic in the Middle West, the Cumberland Road and the Erie Canal, coöperating respectively with Ohio River and Lake Erie steamboats, were of the utmost importance. The national spirit, said to have arisen from the second war with England, had its clearest manifestation in the throwing of a great macadamized roadway across the Alleghanies to the Ohio River and the digging of the Erie

Canal through the swamps and wildernesses of New York.

Both of these pathways were essentially the fruition of the doctrine to which Washington gave wide circulation in his letter to Harrison in 1784, wherein he pictured the vision of a vast Republic united by commercial chains. Both were essentially Western enterprises. The highway was built to fulfil the promise which the Government had made in 1802 to use a portion of the money accruing from the sale of public lands in Ohio in order to connect that young State with Atlantic waters. It was proposed to build the canal, according to one early plan, with funds to be obtained by the sale of land in Michigan. So firmly did the promoters believe in the national importance of this project that subscriptions, according to another plan, were to be solicited as far afield as Vermont in the North and Kentucky in the Southwest. All that Washington had hoped for, and all that Aaron Burr is supposed to have been hopeless of, were epitomized in these great works of internal improvement. They bespoke coöperation of the highest existing types of loyalty, optimism, financial skill, and engineering ability.

Yet, on the other hand, the contrasts between

these undertakings were great. The two enterprises, one the work of the nation and the other that of a single State, were practically contemporaneous and were therefore constantly inviting comparison. The Cumberland Road was, for its day, a gigantic government undertaking involving problems of finance, civil engineering, eminent domain, state rights, local favoritism, and political machination. Its purpose was noble and its successful construction a credit to the nation; but the paternalism to which it gave rise and the conflicts which it precipitated in Congress over questions of constitutionality were remembered soberly for a century. The Erie Canal, after its projectors had failed to obtain national aid, became the undertaking of one commonwealth conducted, amid countless doubts and jeers, to a conclusion unbelievably successful. As a result many States, foregoing Federal aid, attempted to duplicate the successful feat of New York. In this respect the northern canal resembled the Lancaster Turnpike and tempted scores of States and corporations to expenditures which were unwise in circumstances less favorable than those of the fruitful and strategic Empire State.

In the conception of both the roadway and the canal, it should be noted, the old idea of making use of navigable rivers still persisted. The act foreshadowing the Cumberland Road, passed in 1802, called for "making public roads leading from the navigable waters emptying into the Atlantic, to the Ohio, to said State Ohio and through the same"; and Hawley's original plan was to build the Erie Canal from Utica to Buffalo using the Mohawk from Utica to the Hudson.

Historic Cumberland, in Maryland, was chosen by Congress as the eastern terminus of the great highway which should bind Ohio to the Old Thirteen. Commissioners were appointed in 1806 to choose the best route by which the great highway could reach the Ohio River between Steubenville, Ohio and the mouth of Grave Creek; but difficulties of navigation in the neighborhood of the Three Sister Islands near Charlestown, or Wellsburg, West Virginia, led to the choice of Wheeling, farther down, as a temporary western terminus.

The route selected was an excellent compromise between the long standing rival claims of Pennsylvania, Maryland, and Virginia to the trade of the West. If Baltimore and Alexandria were to be better served than Philadelphia, the advantage was slight; and Pennsylvania gained compensation, ere the State gave the National Government permission to build the road within its limits, by dictating that it should pass through Uniontown and Washington. In this way Pennsylvania obtained, without cost, unrivaled advantages for a portion of the State which might otherwise have been long neglected.

The building of the road, however satisfactory in the main, was not undertaken without arousing many sectional and personal hopes and prejudices and jealousies, of which the echoes still linger in local legends today. Land-owners, mine-owners, factory-owners, innkeepers and countless towns-men and villagers anxiously watched the course of the road and were bitterly disappointed if the new sixty-four-foot thoroughfare did not pass immediately through their property. On the other hand, promoters of toll and turnpike companies, who had promising schemes and long lists of share-holders, were far from eager to have their property taken for a national road. No one believed that, if it proved successful, it would be the only work of its kind, and everywhere men looked for the construction of government highways out of the overflowing wealth of the treasury within the next few years.

In April, 1811, the first contracts were let for

building the first ten miles of the road from its eastern terminus and were completed in 1812. More contracts were let in 1812, 1813, and 1815. Even in those days of war when the drain on the national treasury was excessive, over a quarter of a million dollars was appropriated for the construction of the road. Onward it crawled, through the beautiful Cumberland gateway of the Potomac, to Big Savage and Little Savage Mountains, to Little Pine Run (the first "Western" water), to Red Hill (later called "Shades of Death" because of the gloomy forest growth), to high-flung Negro Mountain at an elevation of 2325 feet, and thence on to the Youghiogheny, historic Great Meadows, Braddock's Grave, Laurel Hill, Uniontown, and Brownsville, where it crossed the Monongahela. Thence, on almost a straight line, it sped by way of Washington to Wheeling. Its average cost was upwards of thirteen thousand dollars a mile from the Potomac to the Ohio. The road was used in 1817, and in another year the mail coaches of the United States were running from Washington to Wheeling, West Virginia. Within five years one of the five commission houses doing business at Wheeling is said to have handled over a thousand wagons carrying freight of nearly two tons each.

The Cumberland Road at once leaped into a position of leadership, both in volume of commerce and in popularity, and held its own for two famous decades. The pulse of the nation beat to the steady throb of trade along its highway. Maryland at once stretched out her eager arms, along stone roads, through Frederick and Hagerstown to Cumberland, and thus formed a single route from the Ohio to Baltimore. Great stagecoach and freight lines were soon established, each patronizing its own stage house or wagon stand in the thriving towns along the road. The primitive box stage gave way to the oval or football type with curved top and bottom, and this was displaced in turn by the more practical Concord coach of national fame. The names of the important stagecoach companies were quite as well known, a century ago, as those of our great railways today. Chief among them were the *National*, *Good Intent*, *June Bug*, and *Pioneer* lines. The coaches, drawn by four and sometimes six horses, were usually painted in brilliant colors and were named after eminent statesmen. The drivers of these gay chariots were characters quite as famous locally as the personages whose names were borne by the coaches. Westover and his record of forty-five minutes for the twenty miles between Uniontown and Brownsville, and "Red" Bunting, with his drive of a hundred and thirty-one miles in twelve hours with the declaration of war against Mexico, will be long famous on the curving stretches of the Cumberland Road.

Although the freight and express traffic of those days lacked the picturesqueness of the passenger coaches, nothing illustrates so conclusively what the great road meant to an awakening West as the long lines of heavy Conestogas and rattling express wagons which raced at "unprecedented" speed across hill and vale. Searight, the local historian of the road, describes these large, broad-wheeled wagons covered with white canvas as

visible all the day long, at every point, making the highway look more like a leading avenue of a great city than a road through rural districts. . . . I have staid over night with William Cheets on Nigger [Negro] Mountain when there were about thirty six-horse teams in the wagon yard, a hundred Kentucky mules in an adjoining lot, a thousand hogs in their enclosures, and as many fat cattle in adjoining fields. The music made by this large number of hogs eating corn on a frosty night I shall never forget. After supper and attention to the teams, the wagoners would gather in the bar-room and listen to the music on the violin furnished by one of their fellows, have a Virginia hoe-down, sing songs, tell anecdotes, and hear the experiences of drivers and drovers from all points of the road, and, when it was all over, unroll their beds, lay them down on the floor before the bar-room fire side by side, and sleep with their feet near the blaze as soundly as under the parental roof.

Meanwhile New York, the other great rival for Western trade, was intent on its own darling project, the Erie Canal. In 1808, three years before the building of the Cumberland Road, Joshua Forman offered a bill in favor of the canal in the Legislature of New York. In plain but dignified language this document stated that New York possessed "the best route of communication between the Atlantic and western waters," and that it held "the first commercial rank in the United States." The bill also noted that, while "several of our sister States" were seeking to secure "the trade of that wide extended country," their natural advantages were "vastly inferior." Six hundred dollars was the amount appropriated for a brief survey, and Congress was asked to vote aid for the construction of the "Buffalo-Utica Canal." The matter was widely talked about but action was delayed. Doubt as to the best route to be pursued caused some discussion. If the western terminus were to be located on Lake Ontario at the mouth of the Oswego, as some advocated, would produce not make its way to Montreal instead of to New York? In 1810 a new committee was appointed and, though their report favored the paralleling of the course of the Mohawk and Oswego rivers, their engineer, James Geddes, gave strength to the party which believed a direct canal would best serve the interests of the State. It is worth noting that Livingston and Fulton were added to the committee in 1811.

The hopes of outside aid from Congress and adjacent States met with disappointment. In vain did the advocates of the canal in 1812 plead that its construction would promote "a free and general intercourse between different parts of the United States, tend to the aggrandizement and prosperity of the country, and consolidate and strengthen the Union." The plan to have the Government subsidize the canal by vesting in the State of New York four million acres of Michigan land brought out a protest from the West which is notable not so much because it records the opposition of this section as because it illustrates the shortsightedness of most of the arguments raised against the New York enterprise. The purpose of the canal, the detractors asserted, was to build up New York City to the detriment of Montreal, and the navigation of Lake Ontario, whose beauty they touchingly described, was to be abandoned for a "narrow, winding obstructed canal . . . for an expense which arithmetic dares not approach.". It was, in their minds, unquestionably a selfish object, and they believed that "both correct science, and the dictates of patriotism and philanthropy [should] lead to the adoption of more liberal principles." It was a shortsighted object, "predicated on the eternal adhesion of the Canadas to England." It would never give satisfaction since trade would always ignore artificial and seek natural routes. The attempting of such comparatively useless projects would discourage worthy schemes, relax the bonds of Union, and depress the national character. But though these Westerners thus misjudged the possibilities of the Erie Canal, we must doff our hats to them for their foresight in suggesting that, instead of aiding the Erie Canal, the nation ought to build canals at Niagara Falls and Panama!

The War of 1812 suspended all talk of the canal, but the subject was again brought up by Judge Platt in the autumn of 1816. With alacrity strong men came to the aid of the measure. De Witt

Clinton's *Memorial* of 1816 addressed to the State Legislature may well rank with Washington's letter to Harrison in the documentary history of American commercial development. It sums up the geographical position of New York with reference to the Great Lakes and the Atlantic, her relationship to the West and to Canada, the feasibility of the proposed route from an engineering standpoint, the timeliness of the moment for such a work of improvement, the value that the canal would give to the state lands of the interior, and the trade that it would bring to the towns along its pathway.

The Erie Canal was born in the Act of April 14, 1817, but the decision of the Council of Revision, which held the power of veto, was in doubt. An anecdote related by Judge Platt tends to prove that fear of another war with England was the straw that broke the camel's back of opposition. Acting-Governor Taylor, Chief Justice Thompson, Chancellor Kent, Judge Yates, and Judge Platt composed the Council. The two first named were open opponents of the measure; Kent, Yates, and Platt were warm advocates of the project, but one of them doubted if the time was ripe to undertake it.

Taylor opposed the canal on the ground that the late treaty with England was a mere truce and that the resources of the State should be husbanded against renewed war.

"Do you think so, Sir?" Chancellor Kent is said to have asked the Governor.

"Yes, Sir," was the reported reply. "England will never forgive us for our victories, and, my word for it, we shall have another war with her within two years."

The Chancellor rose to his feet with determination and sealed the fate of the great enterprise in a word.

"If we must have war," he exclaimed, "I am in favor of the canal and I cast my vote for this bill."

On July 4, 1817, work was formally inaugurated at Rome with simple ceremonies. Thus the year 1817 was marked by three great undertakings: the navigation of the Mississippi River upstream and down by steamboats, the opening of the national road across the Alleghany Mountains, and the beginning of the Erie Canal. No single year in the early history of the United States witnessed three such important events in the material progress of the country.

What days the ancient "Long House of the Iroquois" now saw! The engineers of the Cumberland Road, now nearing the Ohio River, had enjoyed the advantage of many precedents and examples; but the Commissioners of the Erie Canal had been able to study only such crude examples of canal-building as America then afforded. Never on any continent had such an inaccessible region been pierced by such a highway. The total length of the whole network of canals in Great Britain did not equal that of the waterway which the New Yorkers now undertook to build. The lack of roads, materials, vehicles, methods of drilling and efficient business systems was overcome by sheer patience and perseverance in experiment. The frozen winter roads saved the day by making it possible to accumulate a proper supply of provisions and materials. As tools of construction, the plough and scraper with their greater capacity for work soon supplanted the shovel and the wheelbarrow, which had been the chief implements for such construction in Europe. Strange new machinery born of Mother Necessity was now heard groaning in the dark swamps of New York. These giants, worked by means of a cable, wheel, and endless screw, were made to hoist

9

green stumps bodily from the ground and, without the use of axe, to lay trees prostrate, root and branch. A new plough was fashioned with which a yoke of oxen could cut roots two inches in thickness well beneath the surface of the ground.

Handicaps of various sorts wore the patience of commissioners, engineers, and contractors. Lack of snow during one winter all but stopped the work by cutting off the source of supplies. Pioneer ailments, such as fever and ague, reaped great harvests, incapacitated more than a thousand workmen at one time and for a brief while stopped work completely.

For the most part, however, work was carried on simultaneously on all the three great links or sections into which the enterprise was divided. Local contractors were given preference by the commissioners, and three-fourths of the work was done by natives of the State. Forward up the Mohawk by Schenectady and Utica to Rome, thence bending southward to Syracuse, and from there by way of Clyde, Lyons, and Palmyra, the canal made its way to the giant viaduct over the Genesee River at Rochester. Keeping close to the summit level on the dividing ridge between Lake Ontario streams and the Valley of the Tonawanda, the line ran to Lockport, where a series of locks placed the canal on the Lake Erie level, 365 miles from and 564 feet above Albany. By June, 1823, the canal was completed from Rochester to Schenectady; in October boats passed into the tidewaters of the Hudson at Albany; and in the autumn of 1825 the canal was formally opened by the passage of a triumphant fleet from Lake Erie to New York Bay. Here two kegs of lake water were emptied into the Atlantic, while the Governor of the State of New York spoke these words:

This solemnity, at this place, on the first arrival of vessels from Lake Erie, is intended to indicate and commemorate the navigable communication, which has been accomplished between our Mediterranean Seas and the Atlantic Ocean, in about eight years, to the extent of more than four hundred and twenty-five miles, by the wisdom, public spirit, and energy of the people of the State of New York; and may the God of the Heavens and the Earth smile most propitiously on this work, and render it subservient to the best interests of the human race.

Throughout these last seven years, the West was subconsciously getting ready to meet the East halfway by improving and extending her steamboat operations. Steamboats were first run on the Great Lakes by enterprising Buffalo citizens who, in 1818, secured rights from the Fulton-Livingston monopoly to build the *Walk-in-the-Water*, the first of the great fleet of ships that now whiten the inland seas of the United States. Regular lines of steamboats were now formed on the Ohio to connect with the Cumberland Road at Wheeling, although the steamboat monopoly threatened to stifle the natural development of transportation on Western rivers.

The completion of the Erie Canal — coupled with the new appropriation by Congress for extending the Cumberland Road from the Ohio River to Missouri and the beginning of the Pennsylvania and the Chesapeake and Ohio canals, reveal the importance of these concluding days of the first quarter of the nineteenth century in the annals of American transportation. Never since that time have men doubted the ability of Americans to accomplish the physical domination of their continent. With the conquest of the Alleghanies and of the forests and swamps of the "Long House" by pick and plough and scraper, and the mastery of the currents of the Mississippi by the paddle wheel, the vast plains beyond seemed smaller and the Rockies less formidable. Men now looked forward confidently, with an optimist of these days, to the time "when circulation and association between the Atlantic and Pacific and the Mexican Gulf shall be as free and perfect as they are at this moment in England" between the extremities of that country. The vision of a nation closely linked by well-worn paths of commerce was daily becoming clearer. What further westward progress was soon to be made remains to be seen.

CHAPTER IX

THE DAWN OF THE IRON AGE

DESPITE the superiority of the new iron age that quickly followed the widespreading canal movement, there was a generous spirit and a chivalry in the "good old days" of the stagecoach, the Conestoga, and the lazy canal boat, which did not to an equal degree pervade the iron age of the railroad. When machinery takes the place of human brawn and patience, there is an indefinable eclipse of human interest. Somehow, cogs and levers and differentials do not have the same appeal as fingers and eyes and muscles. The old days of coach and canal boat had a picturesqueness and a comradeship of their own. In the turmoil and confusion and odd mixing of every kind of humanity along the lines of travel in the days of the hurtling coach-and-six, a friendliness, a robust sympathy, a ready interest in the successful and the unfortunate, a knowledge of how the other half lives, and a familiarity

with men as well as with mere places, was common
to all who took the road. As Thackeray so vividly
describes it:

The land rang yet with the tooting horns and rattling
teams of mail-coaches; a gay sight was the road in
those days, before steam-engines arose and flung its
hostelry and chivalry over. To travel in coaches, to
know coachmen and guards, to be familiar with inns
along the road, to laugh with the jolly hostess in the
bar, to chuck the pretty chamber-maid under the chin,
were the delight of men who were young not very long
ago. The road was an institution, the ring was an
institution. Men rallied around them; and, not without a kind of conservatism expatiated on the benefits
with which they endowed the country, and the evils
which would occur when they should be no more: —
decay of British spirit, decay of manly pluck, ruin of
the breed of horses, and so forth and so forth. To give
and take a black eye was not unusual nor derogatory in
a gentleman: to drive a stage-coach the enjoyment, the
emulation, of generous youth. Is there any young fellow
of the present time, who aspires to take the place of a
stoker? One sees occasionally in the country a dismal
old drag with a lonely driver. Where are you, chariot-
eers? Where are you, O rattling *Quicksilver*, O swift
Defiance? You are passed by racers stronger and swifter
than you. Your lamps are out, and the music of your
horns has died away.

Behind this change from the older and more
picturesque days which is thus lamented there lay

potent economic forces and a strong commercial rivalry between different parts of the country. The Atlantic States were all rivals of each other, reaching out by one bold stroke after another across forest, mountain, and river to the gigantic and fruitful West. Step after step the inevitable conquest went on. Foremost in time marched the sturdy pack-horsemen, blazing the way for the heavier forces quietly biding their time in the rear — the Conestogas, the steamboat, the canal boat, and, last and greatest of them all, the locomotive.

Through a long preliminary period the principal center of interest was the Potomac Valley, towards whose strategic head Virginia and Maryland, by river-improvement and road-building, were directing their commercial routes in amiable rivalry for the conquest of the Western trade. Suddenly out from the southern region of the Middle Atlantic States went the Cumberland National Road to the Ohio. New York instantly, in her zone, took up the challenge and thrust her great Erie Canal across to the Great Lakes. In rapid succession, Pennsylvania and Maryland and Virginia, eager not to be outdone in winning the struggle for Western trade, sent their canals into the Alleghanies toward the Ohio.

It soon developed, however, that Baltimore, both

powerful and ambitious, was seriously handicapped. In order to retain her commanding position as the metropolis of Western trade she was compelled to resort to a new and untried method of transportation which marks an era in American history.

It seems plain that the Southern rivals of New York City — Philadelphia, Baltimore, and Alexandria — had relied for a while on the deterring effect of a host of critics who warned all men that a canal of such proportions as the Erie was not practicable, that no State could bear the financial drain which its construction would involve, that theories which had proved practical on a small scale would fail in so large an undertaking, that the canal would be clogged by floods or frozen up for half of each year, and that commerce would ignore artificial courses and cling to natural channels. But the answer of the Empire State to her rivals was the homely but triumphant cry "Low Bridge!" — the warning to passengers on the decks of canal boats as they approached the numerous bridges which spanned the route. When this cry passed into a byword it afforded positive proof that the Erie Canal traffic was firmly established. The words rang in the counting-houses of Philadelphia and out and along the Lancaster and the

Philadelphia-Pittsburgh turnpikes — "Low Bridge! Low Bridge!" Pennsylvania had granted, it has been pointed out, that her Southern neighbors might have their share of the Ohio Valley trade but maintained that the splendid commerce of the Great Lakes was her own peculiar heritage. Men of Baltimore who had dominated the energetic policy of stone-road building in their State heard this alarming challenge from the North. The echo ran "Low Bridge!" in the poor decaying locks of the Potomac Company where, according to the committee once appointed to examine that enterprise, flood-tides "gave the only navigation that was enjoyed." Were their efforts to keep the Chesapeake metropolis in the lead to be set at naught?

There could be but one answer to the challenge, and that was to rival canal with canal. These more southerly States, confronted by the towering ranges of the Alleghanies to the westward, showed a courage which was superb, although, as time proved in the case of Maryland, they might well have taken more counsel of their fears. Pennsylvania acted swiftly. Though its western waterway — the roaring Juniata, which entered the Susquehanna near Harrisburg — had a drop from head to mouth greater than that of the entire New

York canal, and, though the mountains of the
Altoona region loomed straight up nearly three
thousand feet, Pennsylvania overcame the low-
lands by main strength and the mountain peaks by
strategy and was sending canal boats from Philadelphia to Pittsburgh within nine years of the
completion of the Erie Canal.

The eastern division of the Pennsylvania Canal,
known as the Union Canal, from Reading on the
Schuylkill to Middletown on the Susquehanna,
was completed in 1827. The Juniata section was
then driven on up to Hollidaysburg. Beyond the
mountain barrier, the Conemaugh, the Kiskimini-
tas, and the Allegheny were followed to Pittsburgh.
But the greatest feat in the whole enterprise was
the conquest of the mountain section, from Hollidaysburg to Johnstown. This was accomplished
by the building of five inclined planes on each
slope, each plane averaging about 2300 feet in
length and 200 feet in height. Up or down these
slopes and along the intermediate level sections
cars and giant cradles (built to be lowered into
locks where they could take an entire canal boat
as a load) were to be hauled or lowered by horse-
power, and later, by steam. After the plans had
been drawn up by Sylvester Welch and Moncure

Robinson, the Pennsylvania Legislature authorized the work in 1831, and traffic over this aerial route was begun in March, 1834. In autumn of that year, the stanch boat *Hit or Miss*, from the Lackawanna country, owned by Jesse Crisman and captained by Major Williams, made the journey across the whole length of the canal. It rested for a night on the Alleghany summit "like Noah's Ark on Ararat," wrote Sherman Day, "descended the next morning into the Valley of the Mississippi, and sailed for St. Louis."

Well did Robert Stephenson, the famous English engineer, say that, in boldness of design and difficulty of execution, this Pennsylvania scheme of mastering the Alleghanies could be compared with no modern triumph short of the feats performed at the Simplon Pass and Mont Cenis. Before long this line of communication became a very popular thoroughfare; even Charles Dickens "heartily enjoyed" it — in retrospect — and left interesting impressions of his journey over it:

Even the running up, bare-necked, at five o'clock in the morning from the tainted cabin to the dirty deck; scooping up the icy water, plunging one's head into it, and drawing it out, all fresh and glowing with the cold; was a good thing. The fast, brisk walk upon the towing-path, between that time and breakfast, when every vein and artery seemed to tingle with health; the exquisite beauty of the opening day, when light came gleaming off from everything; the lazy motion of the boat, when one lay idly on the deck, looking through, rather than at, the deep blue sky; the gliding on, at night, so noiselessly, past frowning hills, sullen with dark trees, and sometimes angry in one red burning spot high up, where unseen men lay crouching round a fire; the shining out of the bright stars, undisturbed by noise of wheels or steam, or any other sound than the liquid rippling of the water as the boat went on; all these were pure delights.[1]

Dickens also thus graphically depicts the unique experience of being carried over the mountain peaks on the aerial railway:

There are ten inclined planes; five ascending and five descending; the carriages are dragged up the former, and let slowly down the latter, by means of stationary engines; the comparatively level spaces between being traversed, sometimes by horse, and sometimes by engine power, as the case demands. Occasionally the rails are laid upon the extreme verge of a giddy precipice; and looking from the carriage window, the traveler gazes sheer down, without a stone or scrap of fence between, into the mountain depths below. The journey is very carefully made, however; only two carriages traveling together; and while proper precautions are taken, is not to be dreaded for its dangers.

It was very pretty traveling thus, at a rapid pace

[1] *American Notes* (Gadshill Edition), pp. 180–81.

along the heights of the mountain in a keen wind, to look down into a valley full of light and softness; catching glimpses, through the tree-tops, of scattered cabins; children running to the doors; dogs bursting out to bark, whom we could see without hearing; terrified pigs scampering homewards; families sitting out in their rude gardens; cows gazing upward with a stupid indifference; men in their shirt-sleeves looking on at their unfinished houses, planning out tomorrow's work; and we riding onward, high above them, like a whirl-wind. It was amusing, too, when we had dined, and rattled down a steep pass, having no other motive power than the weight of the carriages themselves, to see the engine released, long after us, come buzzing down alone, like a great insect, its back of green and gold so shining in the sun, that if it had spread a pair of wings and soared away, no one would have had occasion, as I fancied, for the least surprise. But it stopped short of us in a very business-like manner when we reached the canal; and, before we left the wharf, went panting up this hill again, with the passengers who had waited our arrival for the means of traversing the road by which we had come.[1]

This Pennsylvania route was likewise famous because it included the first tunnel in America; but with the advance of years, tunnel, planes, and canal were supplanted by what was to become in time the Pennsylvania Railroad, the pride of the State and one of the great highways of the nation.

[1] *Op. cit.*

In the year before Pennsylvania investigated her western water route, a joint bill was introduced into the legislatures of the Potomac Valley States, proposing a Potomac Canal Company which should construct a Chesapeake and Ohio canal at the expense of Maryland, Virginia, and the District of Columbia. The plan was of vital moment to Alexandria and Georgetown on the Potomac, but unless a lateral canal could be built to Baltimore, that city — which paid a third of Maryland's taxes — would be called on to supply a great sum to benefit only her chief rivals. The bitter struggle which now developed is one of the most significant in commercial history because of its sequel.

The conditions underlying this rivalry must not be lost sight of. Baltimore had done more than any other Eastern city to ally herself with the West and to obtain its trade. She had instinctively responded to every move made by her rivals in the great game. If Pennsylvania promoted a Lancaster Turnpike, Baltimore threw out her superb Baltimore-Reisterstown boulevard, though her northern road to Philadelphia remained the slough that Brissot and Baily had found it. If New York projected an Erie Canal, Baltimore successfully championed the building of a Cumberland Road by a governmental godmother. So thoroughly and quickly, indeed, did she link her system of stone roads to that great artery, that even today many well-informed writers seem to be under the impression that the Cumberland Road ran from the Ohio to Washington and Baltimore. Now, with canals building to the north of her and canals to the south of her, what of her prestige and future?

For the moment Baltimore compromised by agreeing to a Chesapeake and Ohio canal which, by a lateral branch, should still lead to her market square. Her scheme embraced a vision of conquest regal in its sweep, beyond that of any rival, and comprehending two ideas worthy of the most farseeing strategist and the most astute politician. It called not only for the building of a transmontane canal to the Ohio but also for a connecting canal from the Ohio to the Great Lakes. Not only would the trade of the Northwest be secured by this means — for this southerly route would not be affected by winter frosts as would those of Pennsylvania and New York — but the good godmother at Washington would be almost certain to champion it and help to build it since the proposed route was so thoroughly interstate in character. With the backing of Maryland, Virginia, Western

Pennsylvania, Ohio, and probably several States bordering the Inland Lakes, government aid in the undertaking seemed feasible and proper.

Theoretically the daring scheme captured the admiration of all who were to be benefited by it. At a great banquet at Washington, late in 1823, the project was launched. Adams, Clay, and Calhoun took the opportunity to ally themselves with it by robustly declaring themselves in favor of widespread internal improvements. Even the godmother smiled upon it for, following Monroe's recommendation, Congress without hesitation voted thirty thousand dollars for the preliminary survey from Washington to Pittsburgh. Quickly the Chesapeake and Ohio Canal Company and the connecting Maryland Canal Company were formed, and steps were taken to have Ohio promote an Ohio and Lake Erie Company.

As high as were the hopes awakened by this movement, just so deep was the dejection and chagrin into which its advocates were thrown upon receiving the report of the engineers who made the preliminary survey. The estimated cost ran towards a quarter of a billion, four times the capital stock of the company; and there were not lacking those who pointed out that the Erie Canal had cost more than double the original appropriation made for it.

The situation was aggravated for Baltimore by the fact that Maryland and Virginia were willing to take half a loaf if they could not get a whole one: in other words, they were willing to build the canal up the Potomac to Cumberland and stop there. Baltimore, even if linked to this partial scheme, would lose her water connection with the West, the one prized asset which the project had held out, and her Potomac Valley rivals would, on this contracted plan, be in a particularly advantageous position to surpass her. But the last blow was yet to come. Engineers reported that a lateral canal connecting the Potomac and Chesapeake Bay was not feasible. It was consequently of little moment whether the Chesapeake and Ohio Canal could be built across the Alleghanies or not, for, even if it could have been carried through the Great Plains or to the Pacific, Baltimore was, for topographical reasons, out of the running.

The men of Baltimore now gave one of the most striking illustrations of spirit and pluck ever exhibited by the people of any city. They refused to accept defeat. If engineering science held a means of overcoming the natural disadvantages of their position, they were determined to adopt that means, come what would of hardship, difficulty, and expenditure. If roads and canals would not serve the city on the Chesapeake, what of the railroad on which so many experiments were being made in England?

The idea of controlling the trade of the West by railroads was not new. As early as February, 1825, certain astute Pennsylvanians had advocated building a railroad to Pittsburgh instead of a canal, and in a memorial to the Legislature they had set forth the theory that a railroad could be built in one-third of the time and could be operated with one-third of the number of employees required by a canal, that it would never be frozen, and that its cost of construction would be less. But these arguments did not influence the majority, who felt that to follow the line of least resistance and to do as others had done would involve the least hazard. But Baltimore, with her back against the wall, did not have the alternative of a canal. It was a leap into the unknown for her or commercial stagnation.

It is regrettable that, as Baltimore began to break this fresh track, she should have had political as well as physical and mechanical obstacles to overcome. The conquest of the natural difficulties alone required superhuman effort and endurance. But Baltimore had also to fight a miserable internecine warfare in her own State, for Maryland immediately subscribed half a million to the canal as well as to the newly formed Baltimore and Ohio Railroad. In rival pageants, both companies broke ground on July 4, 1828, and the race to the Ohio was on. The canal company clung doggedly to the idle belief that their enterprise was still of continental proportions, since it would connect at Cumberland with the Cumberland Road. This exaggerated estimate of the importance of the undertaking shines out in the pompous words of President Mercer, at the time when construction was begun:

There are moments in the progress of time, which are counters of whole ages. There are events, the monuments of which, surviving every other memorial of human existence, eternize the nation to whose history they belong, after all other vestiges of its glory have disappeared from the globe. At such a moment have we now arrived.

This oracular language lacks the simple but winning straightforwardness of the words which Director Morris uttered on the same day near Baltimore

and which prove how distinctly Western the new
railway project was held to be:

We are about opening a channel through which the
commerce of the mighty country beyond the Allegheny must seek the ocean — we are about affording
facilities of intercourse between the East and West,
which will bind the one more closely to the other,
beyond the power of an increased population or
sectional differences to disunite.

The difficulties which faced the Baltimore enthusiasts in their task of keeping their city "on
the map" would have daunted men of less heroic
mold.   Every conceivable trial and test which
nature and machinery could seemingly devise was
a part of their day's work for twelve years —
struggles with grades, locomotives, rails, cars.   As
Rumsey, Fitch, and Fulton in their experiments
with boats had floundered despondently with endless chains, oars, paddles, duck's feet, so now
Thomas and Brown in their efforts to make the
railroad effective wandered in a maze of difficulties
testing out such absurd and impossible ideas as
cars propelled by sails and cars operated by horse
treadmills.   By May, 1830, however, cars on rails,
running by "brigades" and drawn by horses, were
in operation in America.   It was only in this year

that in England locomotives were used with any marked success on the Liverpool and Manchester Railroad; yet in August of this year Peter Cooper's engine, *Tom Thumb*, built in Baltimore in 1829, traversed the twelve miles between that city and Ellicott's Mills in seventy-two minutes. Steel springs came in 1832, together with car wheels of cylindrical and conical section which made it easier to turn curves.

The railroad was just beginning to master its mechanical problems when a new obstacle confronted it in the Potomac Valley. It could not cross Maryland to the Cumberland mountain gateway unless it could follow the Potomac. But its rival, the canal, had inherited from the old Potomac Company the only earthly asset it possessed of any value — the right of way up the Maryland shore. Five years of quarreling now ensued, and the contest, though it may not have seriously delayed either enterprise, aroused much bitterness and involved the usual train of lawsuits and injunctions.

In 1833 the canal company yielded the railroad a right of way through the Point of Rocks — the Potomac chasm through the Blue Ridge wall, just below Harper's Ferry — on condition that the railroad should not build beyond Harper's Ferry until the canal was completed to Cumberland. But probably nothing but the financial helplessness of the canal company could have brought a solution satisfactory to all concerned. A settlement of the long quarrel by compromise was the price paid for state aid, and, in 1835 Maryland subsidized to a large degree both canal and railroad by her famous eight million dollar bill. The railroad received three millions from the State, and the city of Baltimore was permitted to subscribe an equal amount of stock. With this support and a free right of way, the railroad pushed on up the Potomac. Though delayed by the financial disasters of 1837, in 1842 it was at Hancock; in 1851, at Piedmont; in 1852, at Fairmont; and the next year it reached the Ohio River at Wheeling.

Spurred by the enterprise shown by these Southerners, Pennsylvania and New York now took immediate steps to parallel their own canals by railways. The line of the Union Canal in Pennsylvania was paralleled by a railroad in 1834, the same year in which the Allegheny Portage Railway was constructed. New York lines reached Buffalo in 1842. The Pennsylvania Railroad, which was incorporated in 1846, was completed to Pittsburgh in 1854.

It is thus obvious that, with the completion of these lines and the building of the Chesapeake and Ohio Railway through the "Sapphire Country" of the Southern Alleghanies, the new railway era pursued its paths of conquest through the very same mountain passageways that had been previously used by pack-horseman and Conestoga and, in three instances out of four, by the canal boat. If one motors today in the Juniata Valley in Pennsylvania, he can survey near Newport a scene full of meaning to one who has a taste for history. Traveling along the heights on the highway that was once the red man's trail, he can enjoy a wide prospect from this vantage point. Deep in the valley glitters the little Juniata, route of the ancient canoe and the blundering barge. Beside it lies a long lagoon, an abandoned portion of the Pennsylvania Canal. Beside this again, as though some monster had passed leaving a track clear of trees, stretches the right of way of the first "Pennsylvania," and a little nearer swings the magnificent double-tracked bed of the railroad of today. Between these lines of travel may be read the history of the past two centuries of American commerce, for the vital factors in the development of the nation have been the evolution of transportation and its manifold and far-reaching influence upon the expansion of population and commerce and upon the rise of new industries.

Thus all the rivals in the great contest for the trade of the West speedily reached their goal, New York with the Erie and the New York Central, and Pennsylvania and Maryland with the Pennsylvania and the Baltimore and Ohio. But what of this West for whose commerce the great struggle was being waged? When the railheads of these eager Atlantic promoters were laid down at Buffalo on Lake Erie and at Pittsburgh on the Ohio they looked out on a new world. The centaurs of the Western rivers were no less things of the far past than the tinkling bells borne by the ancient ponies of the pack-horse trade. The sons of this new West had their eyes riveted on the commerce of the Great Lakes and the Mississippi Valley. With road, canal, steamboat, and railway, they were renewing the struggle of their fathers but for prizes greater than their fathers ever knew.

New York again proved the favored State. Her Mohawk pathway gave her easiest access to the West and here, at her back door on the Niagara frontier, lay her path by way of the Great Lakes to the North and the Northwest.

CHAPTER X

As one stands in imagination at the early railheads of the West — on the Ohio River at the end of the Cumberland Road, or at Buffalo, the terminus of the Erie Canal — the vision which Washington caught breaks upon him and the dream of a nation made strong by trans-Alleghany routes of commerce. Link by link the great interior is being connected with the sea. Behind him all lines of transportation lead eastward to the cities of the coast. Before him lies the giant valley where the Father of Waters throws out his two splendid arms, the Ohio and the Missouri, one reaching to the Alleghanies and the other to the Rockies. Northward, at the end of the Erie Canal, lies the empire of the Great Lakes, inland seas that wash the shores of a Northland having a coastline longer than that of the Atlantic from Maine to Mexico.

Ships and conditions of navigation were much

154

the same on the lakes as on the ocean. It was therefore possible to imagine the rise of a coasting trade between Illinois and Ohio as profitable as that between Massachusetts and New York. Yet the older colonies on the Atlantic had an outlet for trade, whereas the Great Lakes had none for craft of any size, since their northern shores lay beyond the international boundary. If there had been danger from Spain in the Southwest, what of the danger of Canada's control of the St. Lawrence River and of the trade of the Northwest through the Welland Canal which was to join Lake Ontario to Lake Erie? But in those days the possibility of Canadian rivalry was not treated with great seriousness, and many men failed to see that the West was soon to contain a very large population. The editor of a newspaper at Munroe, New York, commenting in 1827 on a proposed canal to connect Lake Erie with the Mississippi by way of the Ohio, believed that the rate of Western development was such that this waterway could be expected only "some hundred of years hence." Even so gifted a man as Henry Clay spoke of the proposed canal between Lake Michigan and Lake Superior in 1825 as one relating to a region beyond the pale of civilization "if not in the moon." Yet in twenty-five years Michigan, which had numbered one thousand inhabitants in 1812, had gained two hundredfold, and Ohio, Indiana, and Illinois had their hundreds of thousands who were clamoring for ways and means of sending their surplus products to market.

Early in the century representatives of the Fulton-Livingston monopoly were at the shores of Lake Ontario to prove that their steamboats could master the waves of the inland sea and serve commerce there as well as in tidewater rivers. True, the luckless *Ontario*, built in 1817 at Sackett's Harbor, proved unseaworthy when the waves lifted the shaft of her paddle wheels off their bearings and caused them to demolish the wooden covering built for their protection; but the *Walk-in-the-Water*, completed at Black Rock (Buffalo) in August, 1818, plied successfully as far as Mackinac Island until her destruction three years later. Her engines were then inherited by the *Superior* of stronger build, and with the launching of such boats as the *Niagara*, the *Henry Clay*, and the *Pioneer*, the fleet builders of Buffalo, Cleveland, and Detroit proved themselves not unworthy fellow-countrymen of the old seafarers of Salem and Philadelphia.

But how were cargoes to reach these vessels

from the vast regions beyond the Great Lakes?
Those thousands of settlers who poured into the
Northwest had cargoes ready to fill every manner
of craft in so short a space of time that it seems as
if they must have resorted to arts of necromancy.
It was not magic, however, but perseverance that
had triumphed. The story of the creating of the
main lakeward-reaching canals is long and involved.
A period of agitation and campaigning preceded
every such undertaking; and when construction
was once begun, financial woes usually brought dis-
appointing delays. When a canal was completed
after many vicissitudes and doubts, traffic overwhelmed every method provided to handle it:
locks proved altogether too small; boats were inadequate; wharfs became congested; blockades
which occurred at locks entailed long delay. In
the end only lines and double lines of steel rails
could solve the problem of rapid and adequate
transportation, but the story of the railroad
builders is told elsewhere.[1]

Ohio and Illinois caught the canal fever even
before the Erie Canal was completed, and the
Ohio Canal and the Illinois-Michigan Canal saw

[1] See *The Railroad Builders*, by John Moody (in *The Chronicles of
America*).

preliminary surveying done in 1822 and 1824 respectively. Ohio particularly had cause to seek a northern outlet to Eastern markets by way of Lake Erie. The valleys of the Muskingum, Scioto, and Miami rivers were producing wheat in large quantities as early as 1802, when Ohio was admitted to the Union. Flour which brought $3.50 a barrel in Cincinnati was worth $8 in New York. There were difficulties in the way of transportation. Sometimes ice prevented produce and merchandise from descending the Ohio to Cincinnati. At other times merchants of that city had as many as a hundred thousand barrels awaiting a rise in the river which would make it possible for boats to go over the falls at Louisville. As these conditions involved a delay which often seemed intolerable, the project to build canals to Lake Erie met with generous acclaim. A northward route, though it might be blocked by ice for a few months each winter, had an additional value in the eyes of numerous merchants whose wheat, sent in bulk to New Orleans, had soured either in the long delay at Louisville or in the semi-tropical heat of the Southern port.

The Ohio Legislature in 1822 authorized the survey of all possible routes for canals which would give Ohio an outlet for its produce on Lake Erie.

The three wheat zones which have been mentioned
were favored in the proposed construction of two
canals which, together, should satisfy the need of
increased transportation: the Ohio Canal to connect Portsmouth on the Ohio River with Cleveland
on Lake Erie and to traverse the richest parts of
the Scioto and Muskingum valleys, and to the
west the Miami Canal to pierce the fruitful Miami
and Maumee valleys and join Cincinnati with
Toledo. De Witt Clinton, the presiding genius of
the Erie Canal, was invited to Ohio to play god-
father to these northward arteries which should
ultimately swell the profits of the commission
merchants of New York City, and amid the cheers
of thousands he lifted the first spadefuls of earth
in each undertaking.

The Ohio Canal, which was opened in 1833, had
a marked effect upon the commerce of Lake Erie.
Before that date the largest amount of wheat obtained from Cleveland by a Buffalo firm had been a
thousand bushels; but in the first year of its operation the Ohio Canal brought to the village of Cleveland over a quarter of a million bushels of wheat,
fifty thousand barrels of flour, and over a million
pounds of butter and lard. In return, the markets
of the world sent into Ohio by canal in this same

year thirty thousand barrels of salt and above five million pounds of general merchandise.

Ever since the time when the Erie Canal was begun, Canadian statesmen had been alive to the strong bid New York was making for the trade of the Great Lakes. Their answer to the Erie Canal was the Welland Canal, built between 1824 and 1832 and connecting Lake Erie with Lake Ontario by a series of twenty-seven locks with a drop of three hundred feet in twenty-six miles. This undertaking prepared the way for the subsequent opening of the St. Lawrence canal system (183 miles) and of the Rideau system by way of the Ottawa River (246 miles). There was thus provided an ocean outlet to the north, although it was not until 1856 that an American vessel reached London by way of the St. Lawrence.

With the Hudson and the St. Lawrence in the East thus competing for the trade of the Great Lakes, it is not surprising that the call of the Mississippi for improved highways was presently heard. From the period of the War of 1812 onward the position of the Mississippi River in relation to Lake Michigan was often referred to as holding possibilities of great importance in the development of Western commerce. Already the old portage-path links between the Fox and Wisconsin and the Chicago and Illinois rivers had been worn deep by the fur traders of many generations, and with the dawning of the new era enthusiasts of Illinois were pointing out the strategic position of the latter route for a great trade between Lake Michigan and the Gulf of Mexico.   Thus the wave of enthusiasm for canal construction that had swept New York and Ohio now reached Indiana and Illinois.   Indian ownership of land in the latter State for a moment seemed to block the promotion of the proposed Illinois and Michigan Canal, but a handsome grant of a quarter of a million acres by the Federal Government in 1827 came as a signal recognition of the growing importance of the Northwest; and an appropriation for the lighting and improving of the harbor of the little village of Chicago was hailed by ardent promoters as sure proof that the wedding of Lake Michigan and the Mississippi was but a matter of months.

All the difficulties encountered by the advocates of earlier works of this character, in the valleys of the Potomac, the Susquehanna, and the Mohawk, were the portion of these dogged promoters of Illinois.   Here, as elsewhere, there were rival routes and methods of construction, opposition of jealous sections not immediately benefited, estimates which had to be reconsidered and augmented, and so on. The land grants pledged to pay the bonds were at first of small value, and their advance in price depended on the success of the canal itself, which could not be built — unless the State underwrote the whole enterprise — if the lands were not worth the bonds. Thus the argument ran in a circle, and no one could foresee the splendid traffic and receipts from tolls that would result from the completed canal.

The commissioners in charge of the project performed one interesting service in these early days by putting Chicago on the map; but the two terminals, Ottawa on the Illinois and Chicago on Lake Michigan — both plotted in 1830 — were very largely figures of speech at that time. The day of miracles was at hand, however, for the little town of one hundred people at the foot of Lake Michigan. The purchase of the lands of the Potawatomies, the Black Hawk War in 1832, which brought steamboats to Chicago for the first time, and the decision of Illinois in 1836 to pledge her good name in favor of the Illinois and Michigan Canal made Chicago a city of four thousand people by the panic year of 1837. So absorbed were these Chicago folk in the building of their canal and in wresting from their lake firm foothold for a city (reclaiming four hundred feet of lake bed in two years) that the panic affected their town less than it did many a rival. Although the canal enterprise came to an ominous pause in 1842, after the expenditure of five millions, the pledge of the State stood the enterprise in good stead. Local financiers, together with New York and Boston promoters, advanced about a quarter of a million, while French and English bankers, notably Baring Brothers, contributed about three-quarters of a million. With this assistance the work was carried to a successful ending. On April 10, 1848, the first boat passed over the ninety-mile route from Chicago to Ottawa, and the Great Lakes and the Mississippi Basin were united by this Erie Canal of the West. Though its days of greatest value were soon over, no one can exaggerate the importance of this waterway in the growth and prosperity of Chicago between 1848 and 1860. By 1857 Chicago was sending north and south annually by boat over twenty million bushels of wheat and corn.

The awakening of the lands behind Lake Erie, Lake Huron, and Lake Michigan brought forth innumerable demands for roads, canals, and railways to the ports of Buffalo, Cleveland, Toledo, Detroit, Milwaukee, and Chicago. There were actually hundreds of these enterprises undertaken. The development of the land behind Lake Superior was particularly spectacular and important, not only because of its general effect on the industrial world but also because out of it came the St. Mary's River Ship Canal. Nowhere in the zone of the Great Lakes has any region produced such unexpected changes in American industrial and commercial life as did the region of Michigan, Wisconsin, and Minnesota contributory to Lake Superior. If, as the story goes, Benjamin Franklin said, when he drew at Paris the international boundary line through Lake Superior, that this was his greatest service to America, he did not exaggerate. The line running north of Isle Royale and thence to the Lake of the Woods gave the United States the lion's share of that great inland seaboard and the inestimably rich deposits of copper and iron that have revolutionized American industry.

From earliest days rumors of deposits of bright copper in the land behind Lake Superior had been reported by Indians to fur traders who in turn had passed the story on to fur company agents and thus to the outside world. As a result of her "Toledo

War" — as her boundary dispute was called —
Michigan had reluctantly accepted the northern
peninsula lying between Lake Superior and Lake
Michigan in lieu of the strip of Ohio territory which
she believed to be hers. If Michigan felt that she
had lost by this compromise, her state geologist,
Douglass Houghton, soon found a splendid jewel
in the toad's head of defeat, for the report of his
survey of 1840 confirmed the story of the existence
of large copper deposits, and the first rush to El
Dorado followed.   Amid the usual chaos, conflict,
and failure incident to such stampedes, order and
system at last triumphed and the richest copper
mines of the New World were uncovered.   Then
came the unexpected finding of the mammoth iron-
ore beds by William A. Burt, inventor of the solar
compass.   The circumstance of this discovery is of
such national importance that a contemporary description by a member of Burt's party which was
surveying a line near Marquette, Michigan, is
worth quoting:

I shall never forget the excitement of the old gentleman when viewing the changes of the variation.   He
kept changing his position to take observations, all
the time saying "How would they survey this country
without my compass" and "What could be done here

without my compass." At length the compassman called for us all to "come and see a variation which will beat them all." As we looked at the instrument, to our astonishment, the north end of the needle was traversing a few degrees to the south west. Mr. Burt called out "Boys, look around and see what you can find." We all left the line, some going to the east, some going to the west, and all of us returned with specimens of iron ore.

But it was not enough that this Aladdin's Land in the Northwest should revolutionize the copper and steel industry of the world, for as soon as the soil took to its bosom an enterprising race of agriculturists it bade fair to play as equally important a part in the grain industry. Copper and iron no less came out of the blue of this cold northern region than did the mighty crops of Minnesota wheat, corn, and oats. In the decade preceding the Civil War the export of wheat from Lake Superior rose from fourteen hundred bushels to three and a quarter millions of bushels, while in 1859 nearly seven million bushels of corn and oats were sent out to the world.

The commerce of Lake Superior could not await the building of a canal around the foaming rapids of the St. Mary's River, its one outlet to the lower lakes. In the decade following the discovery of

copper and iron more than a dozen ships, one even
of as much as five hundred tons, were hauled bodily
across the portage between Lake Huron and Lake
Superior.   The last link of navigation in the Great
Lake system, however, was made possible in 1852
by a grant by Congress of 750,000 acres of Michigan land.   Although only a mile in length, the
work proved to be of unusual difficulty since the
pathway for the canal had to be blasted throughout practically its whole length out of solid rock.
It was completed in 1855, and the princely empire
"in the moon" was in a position to make its terms
with the coal fields of Pennsylvania and to usher in
the iron age of transportation and construction.

It is only in the light of this awakening of the
lands around the Great Lakes that one can see
plainly the task which fell to the lot of the successors of the frail *Walk-in-the-Water* and sturdier
Superior of the early twenties.   For the first fifteen
years the steamboat found its mission in carrying
the thousands of emigrants pouring into the Northwest, a heterogeneous multitude which made the
Lake Erie boats seem, to one traveler at least,
filled with "men, women and children, beds, cradles, kettles, and frying pans."   These craft were
built after the pattern of the *Walk-in-the-Water* —

side-wheelers with a steering wheel at the stern. No cabins or staterooms on deck were provided; and amid such freight as the thriving young towns provided were to be found the twenty or thirty cords of wood which the engines required as fuel.

The second period of steamboating began with the opening of the Ohio Canal and the Welland Canal about 1834 and extended another fifteen years to the middle of the century, when it underwent a transformation owing to the great development of Chicago, the completion of the Illinois and Michigan and St. Mary's canals, and the new railways. This second period was marked by the building of such steamers as the *Michigan*, the *Great Western*, and the *Illinois*. These were the first boats with an upper cabin and were looked upon with marked suspicion by those best acquainted with the severe storms upon the Great Lakes. The *Michigan*, of 475 tons, built by Oliver Newberry at Detroit in 1833, is said to have been the first ship of this type. These boats proved their seaworthiness and caused a revolution in the construction of lake craft. Later in this period freight transportation saw an equally radical advance with the building of the first propellers. The sloop-rigged *Vandalia*, built by Sylvester Doolittle at Oswego on Lake Ontario in 1841–42, was the first of the propeller type and was soon followed by the *Hercules*, the *Samson*, and the *Detroit*.

One very great handicap in lake commerce up to this time had been the lack of harbors. Detroit alone of the lake ports was distinctly favored in this respect. The harbors of Buffalo, Cleveland, Milwaukee, and Chicago were improved slowly, but it was not until the great Chicago convention of 1846 that the nation's attention was focused on the needs of Western rivers and harbors, and there dawned a new era of lighthouses and buoys, breakwaters and piers, and dredged channels. Another handicap to the volume of business which the lake boats handled in the period just previous to the Civil War was the inadequacy of the feeders, the roads, riverways, and canals. The Erie Canal was declared too small almost before the cries of its virulent opponents had died away, and the enlargement of its locks was soon undertaken. The same thing proved true of the Ohio and Illinois canals. The failure of the Welland Canal was similarly a very serious handicap. Although its locks were enlarged in 1841, it was found by 1850 that despite the improvements it could not admit more than about one-third of the grain-carrying boats, while only one in four of the new propellers could enter its locks.

As late as the middle forties men did not in the least grasp the commercial situation which now confronted the Northwest nor could they foresee that the land behind the Great Lakes was about to deluge the country with an output of produce and manufactures of which the roads, canals, ships, wharfs, or warehouses in existence could handle not a tenth part. They did not yet understand that this trade was to become national. It was well on in the forties before the Galena lead mines, for instance, were given up as the terminal of the Illinois Central Railroad and the main line was directed to Chicago. The middle of the century was reached before the Lake Shore was considered at Cleveland or Chicago as important commercially as the neighboring portage paths which by the Ordinance of 1787 had been created "common highways forever free." The idea of joining Buffalo, Cleveland, and Chicago with the interior — an idea as old as the Indian trails thither — still dominated men's minds even in the early part of the railroad epoch. Chicago desired to be connected with Cairo, the ice-free port on the Mississippi; and Cleveland was eager to be joined to Columbus

and Cincinnati.   The enthusiastic railway promoters of Ohio, Indiana, and Illinois drew splendid
plans for uniting all parts of those States by railway lines; but the strategic position of the cities on
the continental alignment from New York to the
Pacific by way of South Pass never came within their horizon.   The ten million dollar Illinois
scheme did not even contemplate a railway running eastward from Chicago.   But the future of
the commerce of the Great Lakes depended absolutely upon this development.   There was no hope
of any canals being able to handle the traffic of the
mighty empire which was now awake and fully
conscious of its power.   The solution lay in joining
the cities to each other and to the Atlantic world
markets by iron rails running east and west.

This railroad expansion is what makes the last
decade before the Civil War such a remarkable
series of years in the West.   In the half decade,
1850–55, the Baltimore and Ohio and Pennsylvania railways reached the Ohio River; the links
of the present Lake Shore system between Buffalo
and Chicago by way of Cleveland and Toledo were
constructed; and the Pennsylvania line was put
through from Pittsburgh to Chicago.   The place
of the lake country on the continental alignment

and the imperial situation of Chicago, and later of Omaha, came to be realized. The new view transformed men's conceptions of every port on the Great Lakes in the chain from Buffalo to Chicago. At a dozen southern ports on Ontario, Erie, Huron, and Michigan, commerce now touched the swiftest and most economical means of transcontinental traffic. This development culminated in the miracle we call Chicago. In 1847 not a line of rail entered the town; its population then numbered about twenty-five thousand and its property valuation approximated seven millions. Ten years later four thousand miles of railway connected with all four points of the compass a city of nearly one hundred thousand people, and property valuation had increased five hundred per cent. The growth of Buffalo, Cleveland, and Detroit during this period was also phenomenal.

When the crisis of 1861 came, the service performed by the *Walk-in-the-Water* and her successors was seen in its true light. The Great Lakes as avenues of migration had played a providential part in filling a northern empire with a proud and loyal race; from farm and factory regiment on regiment marched forth to fight for unity; from fields without number produce to sustain a nation on

trial poured forth in abundance; enormous quantities of iron were at hand for the casting of cannon
and cannon balls; and, finally, pathways of water
and steel were in readiness in the nick of time
to carry these resources where they would count
tremendously in the four long years of conflict.

CHAPTER XI

Two great fields of service lay open before those who were to achieve by steam the mastery of the inland waterways. On the one hand the cotton kingdom of the South, now demanding great stores of manufactured goods, produce, and machinery, was waiting to be linked to the valleys and industrial cities of the Middle West; and, on the other hand, along those great eastward and westward rivers, the Ohio and Missouri, lay the commerce of the prairies and the Great Plains. But before the steamboat could serve the inland commerce of the West, it had to be constructed on new lines. The craft brought from the seaboard were of too deep draft to navigate shallow streams which ran through this more level country.

The task of constructing a great inland river marine to play the dual rôle of serving the cotton empire and of extending American migration and commerce into the trans-Mississippi region was solved by Henry Shreve when he built the *Washington* at Wheeling in 1816. Shreve was the American John Hawkins. Hawkins, that sturdy old admiral of Elizabethan days, took the English ship of his time, trimmed down the high stern and poop decks, and cut away the deep-lying prow and stern, after the fashion of our modern cup defenders, and in a day gave England the key to sea mastery in the shape of a new ship that would take sail and answer her rudder beyond anything the maritime world until then had known. Shreve, like Hawkins, flagrantly ignoring the conventional wisdom of his day and craft, built the *Washington* to sail *on* the water instead of *in* it, doing away altogether with a hold and supplying an upper deck in its place.

To few inventors, indeed, does America owe a greater debt of thanks than to this Ohio River shipbuilder. A dozen men were on the way to produce a *Clermont* had Fulton failed; but Shreve had no rival in his plan to build a flat-bottomed steamboat. The remarkable success of his design is attested by the fact that in two decades the boats built on his model outweighed in tonnage all the ships of the Atlantic seaboard and Great Lakes combined. Immediately the Ohio became in effect the western extension of the great national highway and opened an easy pathway for immigration to the eastern as well as the western lands of the Mississippi Basin. The story goes that an old phlegmatic negro watched the approach of one of the first steamboats to the wharf of a Southern city. Like many others, he had doubted the practicability of this new-fangled Yankee notion. The boat, however, came and went with ease and dispatch. The old negro was converted. "By golly," he shouted, waving his cap, "the Mississippi's got her Massa now."

The Mississippi had indeed found her master, but only by slow degrees and after intervals of protracted rebellion did she succumb to that master. Luckily, however, there was at hand an army of unusual men — the "alligator-horses" of the flatboat era — upon whom the steamboat could call with supreme confidence that they would not fail. Theodore Roosevelt has said of the Western pioneers that they "had to be good and strong — especially, strong." If these men upon whom the success of the steamboat depended were not always good, they were beyond any doubt behemoths in strength.

The task before them, however, was a task worthy

THE STEAMER "YELLOWSTONE," ON THE MISSOURI
RIVER

The first vessel that successfully navigated the river; built and operated by the American Fur Company. Engraving after a drawing by Charles Bodmer, in *Travels in the Interior of North America*. In the New York Public Library.

THE STEAMER "YELLOW STONE" ON THE MISSOURI RIVER

The first vessel that successfully navigated the river built and operated by the American Fur Company. Engraving after a drawing by Charles Bodmer, in *Travels in the Interior of North America*. In the New York Public Library

Bravure, Anderson—Lamb, Lo N.Y.

of Hercules. The great river boldly fought its conquerors, asking and giving no quarter, biding its time when opposed by the brave but crushing the fearful on sight. In one respect alone could it be depended upon — it was never the same. It is said to bring down annually four hundred million tons of mud, but its eccentricity in deciding where to wash away and where to deposit its load is still the despair of river pilots. The great river could destroy islands and build new ones overnight with the nonchalance of a child playing with clay. It could shorten itself thirty miles at a single lunge. It could move inland towns to its banks and leave river towns far inland. It transferred the town of Delta, for instance, from three miles below Vicksburg to two miles above it. Men have gone to sleep in one State and have wakened unharmed in another, because the river decided in the night to alter the boundary line. In this way the village of Hard Times, the original site of which was in Louisiana, found itself eventually in Mississippi. Were La Salle to descend the river today by the route he traversed two and a half centuries ago, he would follow dry ground most of the way, for the river now lies practically everywhere either to the right or left of its old course.

12

If the Mississippi could perform such miracles upon its whole course without a show of effort, what could it not do with the little winding canal through its center called by pilots the "channel"? The flatboatmen had laboriously acquired the art of piloting the commerce of the West through this mazy, shifting channel, but as steamboats developed in size and power the man at the wheel had to become almost a superman. He needed to be. He must know the stage of water anywhere by a glance at the river banks. He must guess correctly the amount of "fill" at the head of dangerous chutes, detect bars "working down," distinguish between bars and "sand reefs" or "wind reefs" or "bluff reefs" by night as well as by day, avoid the "breaks" in the "graveyard" behind Goose Island, navigate the Hat Island chutes, or find the "middle crossing" at Hole-in-the-Wall. He must navigate his craft in fogs, in storms, in the face of treacherous winds, on black nights, with thousands of dollars' worth of cargo and hundreds of lives at stake.

As the golfer knows each knoll and tuft of grass on his home links, so the pilot learned his river by heart. Said one of these pilots to an apprentice:

You see this has got to be learned. . . . A clear starlight night throws such heavy shadows that if you didn't know the shape of a shore perfectly you would claw away from every bunch of timber because you would take the black shadow of it for a solid cape; and you see you would be getting scared to death every fifteen minutes by the watch. You would be fifty yards from shore all the time when you ought to be within fifty feet of it. You can't see a snag in one of those shadows, but you know exactly where it is, and the shape of the river tells you when you are coming to it. Then there's your pitch-dark night; the river is a very different shape on a pitch-dark night from what it is on a starlight night. All shores seem to be straight lines, then, and mighty dim ones, too; and you'd *run* them for straight lines only you know better. You boldly drive your boat right into what seems to be a solid, straight wall (you knowing very well that in reality there is a curve there) and that wall falls back and makes way for you. Then there's your gray mist. You take a night when there's one of these grisly, drizzly, gray mists, and then there isn't *any* particular shape to a shore. A gray mist would tangle the head of the oldest man that ever lived. Well, then, different kinds of *moonlight* change the shape of the river in different ways. . . . You only learn the shape of the river; and you learn it with such absolute certainty that you can always steer by the shape that's *in your head* and never mind the one that's before your eyes.[1]

No wonder that the two hundred miles of the Mississippi from the mouth of the Ohio to St. Louis

[1] Mark Twain, *Life on the Mississippi*, pp. 103–04.

in time contained the wrecks of two hundred steamboats.

The river trade reached its zenith between 1840 and 1860, in the two decades previous to the Civil War, that period before the railroads began to parallel the great rivers. It was a time which saw the rise of Ohio, Indiana, Illinois, Missouri, Iowa, and Arkansas, and which witnessed the spread of the cotton kingdom into the Southwest. The story of King Cotton's conquest of the Mississippi South is best told in statistics. In 1811, the year of the first voyage which the *New Orleans* made down the Ohio River, Tennessee, Louisiana, and Mississippi exported five million pounds of cotton. In 1834 these same States exported almost two hundred million pounds of cotton. To take care of this crop and to supply the cotton country, which was becoming wealthy, with the necessaries and luxuries of life, more and more steamboats were needed. The great shipyards situated, because of the proximity of suitable timber, at St. Louis, Cincinnati, and Louisville became busy hives, not since paralleled except by such centers of shipbuilding as Hog Island in 1917–18, during the time of the Great War. The steamboat tonnage of the Mississippi Valley (exclusive of New Orleans) in

the hustling forties exceeded that of the Atlantic
ports (exclusive of New York City) by 15,000 tons.
The steamboat tonnage of New Orleans alone in
1843 was more than double that of New York City.

Those who, if the old story is true, ran in fear to
the hills when the little *New Orleans* went puffing
down the Ohio, in 1811, would have been doubly
amazed at the splendid development in the art of
boat building, could they have seen the stately
Sultana or *Southern Belle* of the fifties sweep swiftly
by. After a period of gaudy ornamentation (1830–
40) steamboat architecture settled down, as has
that of Pullman cars today, to sane and practical
lines, and the boats gained in length and strength,
though they contained less weight of timber. The
value of one of the greater boats of this era would
be about fifty thousand dollars. When Captain
Bixby made his celebrated night crossing at Hat
Island a quarter of a million dollars in ship and cargo
would have been the price of an error in judgment,
according to Mark Twain,[1] a good authority.

The *Yorktown*, built in 1844 for the Ohio-Missis-
sippi trade, was typical of that epoch of inland
commerce. Her length was 182 feet, breadth of
beam 31 feet, and the diameter of wheels 28 feet.

[1] *Op. cit.*, p. 101.

Though her hold was 8 feet in depth, yet she drew
but 4 feet of water light and barely over 8 feet when
loaded with 500 tons of freight. She had 4 boilers,
30 feet long and 42 inches in diameter, double
engines, and two 24-inch cylinders. The state-
room cabin had come in with Captain Isaiah Sellers's *Prairie* in 1836, the first boat with such luxuries ever seen in St. Louis, according to Sellers. The
Yorktown had 40 private cabins. It is interesting
to compare the *Yorktown* with *The Queen of the
West*, the giant British steamer built for the Fal-
mouth-Calcutta trade in 1839. *The Queen of the
West* had a length of 310 feet, a beam of 31 feet, a
draft of 15 feet, and 16 private cabins. The building of this great vessel led a writer in the New York
American to say: "It would really seem that we
as a nation had no interest in this new application
of steam power, or no energy to appropriate it to
our own use." The statement — written in a day
when the Mississippi steamboat tonnage exceeded
that of the entire British Empire — is one of the
best examples of provincial ignorance concerning
the West.

On these steamboats there was a multiplicity of
arrangements and equipments for preventing and
for fighting fire. One of the innovations on the

new boats in this particular was the substitution
of wire for the combustible rope formerly used to
control the tiller, so that even in time of fire the pilot
could "hold her nozzle agin' the bank." Much
of the great loss of life in steamboat fires had been
due to the tiller-ropes being burned and the boats
becoming unmanageable.

The arrival of the railroad at the head of the
Ohio River in the early fifties brought the East
into an immediate touch with the Mississippi Valley unknown before. But however bold railway
engineers were in the face of the ragged ranges
of the Alleghanies, they could not then out-guess
the tricks of the Ohio, the Mississippi, or the Missouri, and railway promoters could not afford to
take chances on having their stations and tracks
unexpectedly isolated, if not actually carried away,
by swirling, yellow floods. The Mississippi, too,
had been known at times to achieve a width of
seventy miles, and tributaries have overflowed
their banks to a proportionate extent. It was
several decades ere the Ohio was paralleled by a
railway, and the Mississippi for long distances even
today has not yet heard the shrill cry of the locomotive. So the steamboat entered its heyday and
encountered little competition. Until the Civil

War the rivers of the West remained the great arteries of trade, carrying grain and merchandise of every description southward and bringing back cotton, rice, and sugar.

The rivalries of the great lines of packets established in these days of the steamboat, however, equaled anything ever known in railway competition, and, in the matter of fast time, became more spectacular than anything of its kind in any line of transportation in our country. With flags flying, boilers heated white with abundance of pine and resin, and bold and skillful pilots at the steering wheels, no sport of kings ever aroused the enthusiasm of hundreds of thousands to such a pitch as did many of the old-time races northward from New Orleans.

The *J. M. White* and her performances stand out conspicuously in the annals of the river. Her builder, familiarly known to a generation of rivermen as Billy King, deserves to rank with Henry Shreve. Commissioned in 1844 to build the *J. M. White* for J. M. Converse of St. Louis, with funds supplied by Robert Chouteau of that city, King proceeded to put into effect the knowledge which he had derived from a close study of the swells made by steamboats when under way. When the

boat was being built in the famous shipyards at
Elizabeth, on the Monongahela, the wheel beams
were set twenty feet farther back than was custom-
ary.   Converse was struck with this unheard-of
radicalism in design, and balked; King was a man
given to few words; he was resolved to throw convention to the winds and trust his judgment; he
refused to build the boat on other lines.   Converse
felt compelled to let Chouteau pass on the question; in time the laconic answer came: "Let King
put the beams where he pleases."

Thus the craft which Converse thought a monstrosity became known far and wide for both its
design and its speed.   In 1844 the *J. M. White*
made the record of three days, twenty-three hours,
and nine minutes between New Orleans and St.
Louis.[1]   Of course the secret of Billy King's success soon became known.   He had placed his paddle wheels where they would bite into the swell

[1] This performance is illustrated by the following comparative table
showing the best records of later years between New Orleans and St.
Louis, a distance estimated in 1844 as 1300 miles but in 1870 as 1218
miles, owing to the action of the river in shortening its course.

Year	Boat	Time
1844	*J. M. White*	3 d. 23 h. 9 m.
1849	*Missouri*	4 d. 19 h. —
1869	*Dexter*	4 d. 9 h. —
1870	*Natchez*	3 d. 21 h. 58 m.
1870	*R. E. Lee*	3 d. 18 h. 14 m.

produced by every boat just under its engines. He
had transformed what had been a handicap into
a positive asset. It is said that he attempted to
shield his prize against competition by destroying
the model of the *J. M. White*, as well as to have refused large offers to build a boat that would beat
her. But it is said also that an exhibition model of
the boat was a cherished possession of E. M. Stan-
ton, Secretary of War, and that it hung in his office
during Lincoln's administration.

The steamboat now extended its service to the
West and North. The ancient fur trade with the
Indians of the upper Mississippi, the Missouri, and
the Arkansas, had its headquarters at St. Louis,
whence the notable band of men engaged in that
trade were reaching out to the Rockies. The roll
includes Ashley, Campbell, Sublette, Manuel Lisa,
Perkins, Hempstead, William Clark, Labadie, the
Chouteaus, and Menard — men of different races
and colors and alike only in their energy, bravery,
and initiative. Through them the village of St.
Louis had grown to a population of four thousand
in 1819, when Major Long's expedition passed up
the Missouri in the first steamboat to ascend that
river. This boat, the *Western Engineer*, was built
at Pittsburgh and was modeled cunningly for its

work.   It was one of the first stern wheelers built
in the West; and the saving in width meant much
on streams having such narrow channels as the Missouri and the Platte, especially when barges were
to be towed.   Then, too, its machinery, which was
covered over or boarded up, was shrouded in mystery.   A fantastic figure representing a serpent's
open mouth contained the exhaust pipe.   If the
New Orleans alarmed the population of the Ohio
Valley, the sensation caused among the red children
of the Missouri at the sight of this gigantic snake
belching fire and smoke must have thoroughly
satisfied the whim of its designer.

The admission of Missouri to statehood and the
independence of Mexico mark the beginning of real
commercial relations between St. Louis and Santa
Fé.   In 1822 Captain William Becknell organized
the first wagon train which left the Missouri (at
Franklin, near Independence) for the long dangerous journey to the Arkansas and on to Santa Fé.
In the following year two expeditions set forth,
carrying out cottons and other drygoods to
exchange for horses, mules, furs, and silver.

Despite the handicaps of Indian opposition and
Mexican tariffs, the Santa Fé trade became an important factor in the growth of St. Louis and the

Missouri River steamboat lines. In 1825 the pathway was "surveyed" from Franklin to San Fernando, then in Mexico. This Santa Fé trade grew from fifteen thousand pounds of freight in 1822 to nearly half a million pounds twenty years later.

By 1826 steamboat traffic up the Missouri began to assume regularity. The navigation was dangerous and difficult because the Missouri never kept even an approximately constant head of water. In times of drought it became very shallow, and in times of flood it tore its wayward course open in any direction it chose. "Of all variable things in creation," wrote a Western editor, "the most uncertain are the action of a jury, the state of a woman's mind, and the condition of the Missouri River." A further handicap, and one which was unknown on the Ohio and rare on the Mississippi, was the lack of forests to supply the necessary fuel. The Missouri, it is true, had its cottonwoods, but in a green state they were poor fuel, and along vast stretches they were not obtainable in any quantity.

The steamboat linked St. Louis with that vital stretch of the river lying between the mouth of the Kansas and the mouth of the Nebraska. From this region the great Western trail ran on to California and Oregon. In the early thirties

Bonneville, Walker, Kelley, and Wyeth successively essayed this Overland Trail by way of the Platte through the South Pass of the Rockies to the Humboldt, Snake, and Columbia rivers. From Independence on the Missouri this famous pathway led to Fort Laramie, a distance of 672 miles; another 300-mile climb brought the traveler through South Pass; and so, by way of Fort Bridger, Salt Lake, and Sutter's Fort, to San Francisco. The route, well known by hundreds of Oregon pioneers in the early forties, became a thoroughfare in the eager days of the Forty-Niners.[1]

The earliest overland stage line to Great Salt Lake was established by Hockaday and Liggett. After the founding of the famous Overland Stage Company by Russell, Majors, and Waddell in 1858, stages were soon ascending the Platte from the steamboat terminals on the Missouri and making the twelve hundred miles from St. Joseph to Salt Lake City in ten days. Stations were established from ten to fifteen miles apart, and the line was soon extended on to Sacramento. The nineteen hundred miles from St. Joseph to Sacramento were made in fifteen days, although the government

[1] For map see *The Passing of the Frontier*, by Emerson Hough (in *The Chronicles of America*).

contract with the company for handling United States mail allowed nineteen days. A host of employees was engaged in this exciting but not very remunerative enterprise—station-agents and helpers, drivers, conductors who had charge of passengers, in addition to mail and express and road agents who acted as division superintendents. In 1862 the Overland Route was taken over by the renowned Ben Holliday, who operated it until the railway was constructed seven years later. Freight was hauled by the same company in wagons known as the "J. Murphy wagons," which were made in St. Louis. These wagons went out from Leavenworth loaded with six thousand pounds of freight each. A train usually consisted of twenty-five wagons and was known, in the vernacular of the plains, as a "bull-outfit"; the drivers were "bull-whackers"; and the wagon master was the "bull-wagon boss."

The old story, however, was repeated again here on the boundless plains of the West. The Western trails streaming out from the terminus of steamboat traffic between Kansas City and Omaha had scarcely time to become well known before the railway conquerors of the Atlantic and Great Lakes regions were planning the conquest of the greater plains and the Rockies beyond. The opening of the Chinese ports in 1844 turned men's minds as never before to the Pacific coast. The acquisition of Oregon within a few years and of California at the close of the Mexican War opened the way for a newspaper and congressional discussion as to whether the first railway to parallel the Santa Fé or the Overland Trail should run from Memphis, St. Louis, or Chicago. The building of the Union Pacific from Omaha westward assured the future of that city, and it was soon joined to Chicago and the East by several lines which were building toward Clinton, Rock Island, and Burlington.

But the construction of a few main lines of railway across the continent could only partially satisfy the commercial needs of the West. True, the overland trade was at once transferred to the railroad, but the enormous equipment of stage and express companies previously employed in westward overland trade was now devoted to joining the railway lines with the vast regions to the north and the south. The rivers of the West could not alone take care of this commerce and for many years these great transportation companies went with their stages and their wagons into the growing Dakota and Montana trade and opened up direct lines of communication to the nearest railway. On the south the cattle industry of Texas came northward into touch with the railways of Kansas. Eventually lateral and trunk lines covered the West with their network of lines and thus obliterated all rivalry and competition by providing unmatched facilities for quick transportation.

In the last days previous to the opening of the first transcontinental railway line a unique method of rapid transportation for mail and light parcels was established when the famous "Pony Express" line was put into operation between St. Joseph and San Francisco in 1860. By relays of horsemen, who carried pouches not exceeding twenty pounds in weight, the time was cut to nine days. The innovation was the new wonder of the world for the time being and led to an outburst on the part of the enthusiastic editor of the St. Joseph *Free Democrat* that deserves reading because it breathes so fully the Western spirit of exultant conquest:

Take down your map and trace the footprints of our quadrupedantic animal: From St. Joseph, on the Missouri, to San Francisco, on the Golden Horn — two thousand miles — more than half the distance across our boundless continent; through Kansas, through Nebraska, by Fort Kearney, along the Platte, by Fort Laramie, past the Buttes, over the Mountains, through the narrow passes and along the steep defiles,

Utah, Fort Bridger, Salt Lake City, he witches Brigham with his swift pony-ship — through the valleys, along the grassy slopes, into the snow, into the sand, faster than Thor's Thialfi, away they go, rider and horse — did you see them? They are in California, leaping over its golden sands, treading its busy streets. The courser has unrolled to us the great American panorama, allowed us to glance at the home of one million people, and has put a girdle around the earth in forty minutes. Verily the riding is like the riding of Jehu, the son of Nimshi for he rideth furiously. Take out your watch. We are eight days from New York, eighteen from London. The race is to the swift. [1]

The lifetime of many and many a man has covered a period longer than that interval of eighty-six years between 1783, when George Washington had his vision of "the vast inland navigation of these United States," and the year 1869, when the two divisions of the Union Pacific were joined by a golden spike at Promontory Point in Utah. In point of time, those eighty-six years are as nothing; in point of accomplishment, they stand unparalleled. When Washington's horse splashed across the Youghiogheny in October, 1784, the boundary lines of the United States were guarded with all the jealousy and provincial selfishness of European kingdoms. But overnight, so to speak, these

[1] Quoted in Inman's *The Great Salt Lake Trail*, p. 171.

limitations became no more than mere geometrical expressions. "Pennamite," "Erie," and "Toledo" wars between the States, suggesting a world of bitterness and recrimination, are remembered today, if at all, only by the cartoonist and the playwright. The ancient false pride in mock values, so cherished in Europe, has quite departed from the provincial areas of the United States, and Americans can fly in a day, unwittingly, through many States. Problems that would have cost Europe blood are settled without turmoil in the solemn cloisters of that American "international tribunal," the Supreme Court, and they appear only as items of passing interest in our newspapers.

In unifying the nation the influence of the Supreme Court has been priceless, for it has given to Americans, in place of the colonial or provincial mind, a continental mind. But great is the debt of Americans to the men who laid the foundations of interstate commerce. No antidote served so well to counteract the poison of clannish rivalry as did their enthusiasm and their constructive energy. These men, dreamers and promoters, were building better than they knew. They thought to overcome mountains, obliterate swamps, conquer stormy lakes, master great rivers and endless plains;

but, as their labors are judged today, the greater service which these men rendered appears in its true light.   They stifled provincialism; they battered down Chinese Walls of prejudice and separatism; they reduced the aimless rivalry of bickering provinces to a businesslike common denominator; and, perhaps more than any class of men, they made possible the wide-spreading and yet united Republic that is honored and loved today.

BIBLIOGRAPHICAL NOTE

THE history of the early phase of American transportation is dealt with in three general works. John Luther Ringwalt's *Development of Transportation Systems in the United States* (1888) is a reliable summary of the general subject at the time. Archer B. Hulbert's *Historic Highways of America*, 16 vols. (1902–1905), is a collection of monographs of varying quality written with youthful enthusiasm by the author, who traversed in good part the main pioneer roads and canals of the eastern portion of the United States; Indian trails, portage paths, the military roads of the Old French War period, the Ohio River as a pathway of migration, the Cumberland Road, and three of the canals which played a part in the western movement, form the subject of the more valuable volumes. The temptation of a writer on transportation to wander from his subject is illustrated in this work, as it is illustrated afresh in Seymour Dunbar's *A History of Travel in America*, 4 vols. (1915). The reader will take great pleasure in this magnificently illustrated work, which, in completer fashion than it has ever been attempted, gives a readable running story of the whole subject for the whole country, despite detours, which some will make around the many pages devoted to Indian relations.

197

For almost every phase of the general topic books, monographs, pamphlets, and articles are to be found in the corners of any great library, ranging in character from such productions as William F. Ganong's *A Monograph of Historic Sites in the Province of New Brunswick* (*Proceedings and Transactions* of the Royal Society of Canada, Second Series, vol. v, 1899) which treats of early travel in New England and Canada, or St. George L. Sioussat's *Highway Legislation in Maryland and its Influence on the Economic Development of the State* (*Maryland Geological Survey*, iii, 1899) treating of colonial road making and legislation thereon, or Elbert J. Benton's *The Wabash Trade Route in the Development of the Old Northwest* (*Johns Hopkins University Studies in Historical and Political Science*, vol. xxi, 1903) and Julius Winden's *The Influence of the Erie Canal upon the Population along its Course* (University of Wisconsin, 1901), which treat of the economic and political influence of the opening of inland water routes, to volumes of a more popular character such as Francis W. Halsey's *The Old New York Frontier* (1901), Frank H. Severance's *Old Trails on the Niagara Frontier* (1903) for the North, and Charles A. Hanna's *The Wilderness Trail*, 2 vols. (1911), and Thomas Speed's *The Wilderness Road* (*The Filson Club Publications*, vol. ii, 1886) for Pennsylvania, Virginia, and Kentucky. The value of Hanna's work deserves special mention.

For the early phases of inland navigation John Pickell's *A New Chapter in the Early Life of Washington* (1856), is an excellent work of the old-fashioned type, while in Herbert B. Adams's *Maryland's Influence upon Land Cessions to the United States* (*Johns Hopkins*

University Studies in Historical and Political Science, Third Series, i, 1885) a master-hand pays Washington his due for originating plans of trans-Alleghany solidarity; this likewise is the theme of Archer B. Hulbert's *Washington and the West* (1905) wherein is printed Washington's *Diary of September, 1784*, containing the first and unexpurgated draft of his classic letter to Harrison of that year. The publications of the various societies for internal improvement and state boards of control and a few books, such as Turner Camac's *Facts and Arguments Respecting the Great Utility of an Extensive Plan of Inland Navigation in America* (1805), give the student distinct impressions of the difficulties and the ideals of the first great American promoters of inland commerce. Elkanah Watson's *History of the . . . Western Canals in the State of New York* (1820), despite inaccuracies due to lapses of memory, should be specially remarked.

For the rise and progress of turnpike building one must remember W. Kingsford's *History, Structure, and Statistics of Plank Roads* (1852), a reliable book by a careful writer. The Cumberland (National) Road has its political influence carefully adjudged by Jeremiah S. Young in *A Political and Constitutional Study of the Cumberland Road* (1904), while the social and personal side is interestingly treated in county history style in Thomas B. Searight's *The Old Pike* (1894). Motorists will appreciate Robert Bruce's *The National Road* (1916), handsomely illustrated and containing forty-odd sectional maps.

The best life of Fulton is H. W. Dickinson's *Robert Fulton, Engineer and Artist: His Life and Works* (1913), while in Alice Crary Sutcliffe's *Robert Fulton and the*

"*Clermont*" (1909), the more intimate picture of a family biography is given. For the controversy concerning the Fulton-Livingston monopoly, note W. A. Duer's *A Course of Lectures on Constitutional Jurisprudence* and his pamphlets addressed to Cadwallader D. Colden. The life of that stranger to success, the forlorn John Fitch, was written sympathetically and after assiduous research by Thompson Westcott in his *Life of John Fitch the Inventor of the Steamboat* (1858). For the pamphlet war between Fitch and Rumsey see Allibone's Dictionary.

The Great Lakes have not been adequately treated. E. Channing and M. F. Lansing's *The Story of the Great Lakes* (1909) is reliable but deals very largely with the routine history covered by the works of Parkman. J. O. Curwood's *The Great Lakes* (1909) is stereotyped in its scope but has certain chapters of interest to students of commercial development, as has also *The Story of the Great Lakes*. The vast bulk of material of value on the subject lies in the publications of the New York, Buffalo, Michigan, Wisconsin, Illinois, and Chicago Historical Societies, whose lists should be consulted. These publications also give much data on the Mississippi River and western commercial development. S. L. Clemens's *Life on the Mississippi* (in his *Writings*, vol. IX, 1869–1909) is invaluable for its graphic pictures of steamboating in the heyday of river traffic. A. B. Hulbert's *Waterways of Western Expansion* (*Historic Highways*, vol. IX, 1903) and *The Ohio River* (1906) give chapters on commerce and transportation. For the beginnings of traffic into the Far West, H. Inman's *The Old Santa Fé Trail* (1897) and *The Great Salt Lake Trail* (1914) may be consulted, together with the publications of the various state historical societies of the trans-Mississippi States.

Various bibliographies on this general subject have been issued by the Library of Congress. Seymour Dunbar gives a good bibliography in his *A History of Travel in America*, 4 vols. (1915). The student will find quantities of material in books of travel, in which connection he would do well to consult Solon J. Buck's *Travel and Description, 1765–1865* (*Illinois State Historical Library Collections*, vol. IX, 1914).

INDEX